Alfred Seiler

From
Hitler's Death Camps
To
Stalin's Gulags

ISBN 978-0-557-36946-1

I dedicate this book to my father,
whom I never understood

Contents

Introduction

My sixty-fifth birthday came and went. From the bits and pieces of my life that I have told, I have been asked a number of times to write it all down so my descendants will not have to guess where their forebears came from. This gives me an opportunity to create a permanent record of the times leading up to the Second World War as seen through the eyes of one of the persecuted.

I will try to be very frank and truthful in describing relatives, friends, certain people and events; therefore, I would like the reader to treat these memoirs as my personal observation and story, so that my criticism should not hurt anybody or cloud any relations in the future.

All you will read here are names, places, things and events the way I remember, with the exception of historical data and some notes jotted down by my father describing some events of his youth. For the rest, I hope that my memory will serve me well.

1. The Twentieth Century

We are blessed — or as the reader will notice, sometimes cursed — to live in a century full of miraculous discoveries, both for the benefit and destruction of man.

I have seen the development of many things that we take for granted today: The automobile, the airplane, radio and television, the computer, the laser beam, supersonic aircraft, men walking on the moon, the atomic bomb and atomic power for peaceful uses, the Salk vaccine and other healing processes, and so much more that it is impossible to record it all.

I have also seen and experienced the rise and fall of Nazism and the rise and fall of Communism, two dangers threatening the very existence of the world and of mankind.

As I write this in 1991, we are experiencing fast-moving political changes.

The name Soviet Union may soon sound as antique as Third Reich or Belgian Congo. Terms like Cold War, Iron Curtain, Berlin Wall, Kremlinology, and East-West Struggle are winding up on the garbage heap of history. Voluminous dictionaries are turning archaic, and all these words will soon look quaint and tiresome to the coming waves of grandchildren whose cultural education began with Big Bird and Barney.

I have also witnessed the creation of the State of Israel, giving Jews a homeland after 2,000 years of dispersion and Diaspora, a mitigating answer to the tragic deaths of six million of our people who were killed by the Germans during the Second World War.

All this and more I have seen and experienced, and when I am called to the highest tribunal, I will just say:

"Lord, I have been through Hell during the Hitler and Stalin years. I deserve to go to Paradise."

Honig ist nicht ohne Bienen
Wer in Kanaan will sein
Muss erst in Aegypten dienen
Und durch Meer und Wüste ziehen

Honey is not without bees
Who wants to be in Canaan
First must toil in Egypt land
And wander through desert and seas

2. Family

To write about my past, my childhood, my years as a teenager growing up in difficult times or as a young adult who survived the Holocaust, I have nothing to base my stories on but my memory.

Father, William Wolf Seiler

The only power or strength that one possesses to put everything on paper is the brain. It is the built-in computer that lets you open or close a small window through which one can see things long buried and forgotten. Sometimes that window opens without warning, turning one's waking moments into dreams — or nightmares.

I was born on February 14, 1926 to a middle-class Jewish family, in Vienna, the capital of the Republic of Austria. My given name is Alfred, although I have been called all my life either Fred or Freddie, or during my "Russian" period, Fredjik.

My father, William Wolf Seiler, had come to Vienna as a child. He was one of 17 children, only five of whom reached adulthood. He attended public and trade schools in this seat of the Hapsburg Empire, where he was "proud to live and to breathe the same air as the emperor." He was a soldier of the Austro-Hungarian monarchy during the years 1914-1918, the years of the First World War, the war that was to end all wars for all times. He was wounded and as a 25 per cent invalid de-mustered from the army.

He had come from Kopyczince, a small town on the (former) Russian-Polish border in the district of Husiatin. Leaving his parents behind, he was brought up by his oldest sister, sixteen years his elder, Anna Dressler. After finishing his schooling, he worked for a textile house in the center of the city called Tuchlauben.

Maternal grandfather, Bernard Glanzmann

I never knew my paternal grandfather, who died before I was born. The Jewish name that was given me, Aaron, was to honor his memory. The family name Seiler was handed down by imperial edict. All Jews living in the Pale — the lands of Eastern Europe where they were settled by Russian tsars — were ordered to adopt names indicating their professions. As a rope maker, my grandfather had to accept this name. Shoemakers would be Schuster, tailors would be Schneider, and so on.

My mother, Chaje Esther (Klara) nee Glanzmann, came to Vienna at an early age. She was born in a small town, Sadowa Wisznia, a whistle-stop between the cities of Lemberg (Lwow) and Prczemisl. Already present in Vienna were her oldest brother, Leo, and her elder sister Amalia (Tante Mollie).

In coming to Vienna, she left behind quite a large family. Besides her parents, father Bernard Glanzmann and mother Deborah (nee Schwartz), there were also five more brothers: Herman, Anschel, Leib, Daniel and Joseph. Originally, there had been 16 children, but the rest never reached adulthood.

My maternal grandfather, Bernard, owned a soap factory, which was next to a large house where most of the remaining members of the clan lived. The buildings, which included stables, were surrounded by a high wooden fence guarded by two big watchdogs named Bossie (barefoot) and Dunay (Danube). In the middle of the property was a well that usually ran dry in the middle of summer.

Once a week, the Polish peasants were permitted to enter the factory grounds and swap produce for soap. There was always excitement and the air seemed to be laden with electricity when the peasant women started arguing about

the value of their eggs or other foodstuff in comparison with the value of soap they got in exchange.

Beyond the buildings and within the perimeter of the surrounding fence was a large garden that supplied the household with all the necessary vegetables and fruit.

My sister Mary and me

I have a clear memory of all these things, although I was there only once on summer vacation when I was about five or six. My sister Mary and I had a good time raiding the garden, eating fruit and drinking the pods of the poppy seeds. We were also free to roam the countryside with the dogs.

On Sunday it was always a treat to watch the Polish people walk by the house on the way to church. They wore magnificent costumes, walking barefoot with their boots slung on their shoulders so as not to damage their proud possession. They would then put the boots on before entering the church.

I remember the town of Sadowa Wisznia that seemed to be a "lifetime of walking" away when grandfather took us to Shul on Shabbes morning.

My parents

But the return home would always be grandiose. Nobody would dare to eat until grandfather would recite the blessing, or on Saturday night would make the Havdala.

My father and mother were married on October 22, 1922. My sister, Mary (Miriam), was born August 24, 1923 — and yours truly on February 14, 1926.

To continue telling my story, I will have to introduce the rest of my family and describe the relationship. I will mark all the people killed by the Nazis with the letter "K," those who died a natural death with the letter "D," and the ones still alive at this writing with the letter "L."

My maternal grandparents, Deborah (D) and Bernard (K) Glanzmann; my uncles Herman (K), Anschel (K), Leib (K), Daniel (D 1999) and Joseph (K); my uncle Leo (D), my mother's sister Amalia-Mollie (K) and my mother (D).

While my grandfather Bernard was the undisputed head of the clan, my grandmother Deborah was the undisputed head of the household. She reigned with two women helpers in the large kitchen where the hearth fire was constantly burning from Saturday night to Friday afternoon.

A large brick oven would be fired up with logs, and when the bricks inside the oven were red hot, the embers would be removed and the bread and the challah would then be baked.

The warmth of the oven would also serve to keep the

My father with his employees

food hot over the Sabbath.

My grandmother Deborah died in 1936 when she was 66.

Leo Glanzmann, my uncle, and Amalia Glanzmann, my aunt, had preceded my mother in coming to Vienna. My mother was born October 2, 1896. After finishing her schooling, she joined my aunt and my uncle in the venture of manufacturing dresses. This was the beginning of Glanzmann, Epstein & Co. The clothing firm was located at 35 Obere Donaustraße in the 2nd district of Vienna and blossomed into a big undertaking, providing a comfortable living for four families.

Leo Glanzmann, my mother's eldest brother, married Regina (D) Glanzmann, a cousin. They had one daughter, Sophie (D), who lived with her husband Naum (L) Zcirulnik in Haifa, Israel. They survived the Holocaust by hiding out in various locations around Lwow and returned to claim their rightful place. Their apartment and belongings were kept in amazingly good order by the interlopers who had taken possession of them.

Leo served in the Austro-Hungarian Army during the First World War, stationed on the Italo-Austrian front as an observer during all 11 battles on the river Isonzo. After the downfall of the monarchy, he neglected to opt for Austrian citizenship and became a citizen of Poland.

My playmate Herby, Irene and Teddy Epstein

Amalia Glanzmann (K) married Isidor Epstein (K). They had three children: Irene (K), Theodor (K) and Herbert (K). Herbert, only one month older than I, was my steady companion and my playmate. Isidor Epstein joined the company that now bore his name, too. He never opted for Austrian citizenship and like his brother-in-law became a citizen of Poland

Also living in Vienna was my father's brother Carl (K) and his wife Ruszia (K). Both were killed in Lodz on October 28, 1941. (Ruszia was Isidor Epstein's sister). They had two children Jenny (K) and Siegfried (D). Siegfried (Fred) was secretly married to Rosa Wahrsager (D) in the late 1920's. As the younger brother, he did not want to announce his marriage until his sister Jenny had gotten married. Jenny (K) married Hans Amschel (K), a dental technician. They had one daughter, Eva (K). They lived in Ottakring, the 16th district of the city, were Hans also had his practice. He loved to hang out with his cronies from the Nazi Party and even testified on their behalf after the 1935 putsch. This he later claimed would protect and exempt him from any excesses against the Jews — until he was thrown out of his apartment and sent to share the fate of all others in a concentration camp.

Tante Anna (K), my father's eldest sister, married Meier (D/K) Dressler, a distant cousin. Being 16 years older than my father, she acted as his surrogate mother and took care of him in his early years. She was born, December 12, 1879 and killed in Maly Trostenez, April 9, 1942.

My Tante Frieda and Max Dressler

Tante Frieda (K) married Max (K) Dressler. She was my father's other sister living in Vienna. This marriage produced two sons, Siegfried (Siggi) (D), and Adolph (Dolphi) (L). Siggi lived in Vienna and was married to Bertha (D), and Dolphi, living in the USA, married Blanka (D). Tante Frieda and Max were killed January 13, 1943 in Theresianstadt. The third sister, Adele (K), lived in the parental house in Poland until the beginning of 1938, when she and her husband Moritz Katz (K) moved with their children Nolo (L) and Renia (L) to Vienna. Back in Poland he smuggled cattle between Russia, Poland and Romania. My father (D), the fifth of the original Seiler siblings, was born on December 19, 1895. This is the family tree as I know it and as far as I can remember.

After I had completed four years of public schooling, I was sent to the first and foremost "Conservative" Jewish gymnasium, the Chajes-Real Gymnasium, the only modern Jewish high-school in Vienna. It was a very demanding school. I had a very hard time just keeping up with the curriculum.

3. Austrian history

While this seemingly prosperous country was keeping its head above the water, unrest and trouble were brewing inside the country and north of the border.

Adolf Hitler had come to power in Germany in early 1933. To understand what was happening in Germany, to understand what lay in store for the Jews, it is necessary to know more about Hitler, the Austrian corporal and second-rate painter who had been unopposed as Germany's absolute dictator.

On January 30, 1933 Hitler was named chancellor of Germany and became head of the coalition government of his National Socialists and the right-wing Nationalist Party. German President Hindenburg and his advisors hoped that Hitler could end the political chaos that had engulfed Germany but that his right-wing ideas could still be restrained.

The Weimar Constitution under which Germany was governed contained a fatal flaw. Emergency provisions allowed the president to usurp the constitutional powers of the state government, suspend the constitutional guarantee of civil liberties and to dissolve the Reichstag (Germany's parliament). The Reichstag could also grant legislative powers to the chancellor. Here were the openings that Hitler needed to seize power.

On February 27, 1933 — less than a month after Hitler became chancellor — the Reichstag building was set afire.

Hitler blamed the Communists and persuaded Hindenburg to invoke emergency powers.

Thousands of Communists as well as Social Democrats, Liberals and a vast majority of the members of the Reichstag were arrested. A shoot-to-kill order encouraged the police to fire on demonstrators.

In the last few days before the scheduled March elections, violent disturbances were created throughout the country by S.A. Storm Troopers, the so-called "brown shirts," who functioned as the paramilitary arm of the Nazi Party. From this chaos of their own creation, the Nazis were able to amass 44 percent of the popular vote.

The Reichstag reconvened and gave Hitler dictatorial powers. As a result, the Weimar Republic was effectively dead, the Reichstag a little more than a rubber stamp. For the next 12 years, Germany would be ruled by the "Führer," freely translated as the "leader."

Hitler moved quickly to consolidate all state powers into his hands and carry out the "Nazification" of German culture. On April 7, 1933 federal states were dissolved and Nazi governors appointed. May 1 was declared a workers' holiday and labor leaders were invited to participate in the parades and celebrations. The next day, trade union leaders were arrested and all labor unions had ceased to exist.

The judiciary was also brought under Nazi control. By early May, a "People's" court was established to try treason cases. Proceedings were secret and there was no way to appeal a verdict, except to Hitler. Death sentences were handed down routinely. Between May and July 1933, all opposing political parties were dissolved. On July 14, 1933 the National Socialist Workers Party (NSDAP) was declared the only political party in Germany.

The same day, the Law for Prevention of Hereditary and Defective Offspring was proclaimed. This law authorized the surgical sterilization of people who were mentally retarded, schizophrenic, alcoholic or genetically diseased.

Hitler soon formed an all-Nazi government dedicated

to his racial beliefs. In addition to the normal government agencies that controlled such functions as transportation, agriculture and banking, agencies were created to control the German people. One of Hitler's main goals was to make Germany "Judenrein," meaning cleansed of Jews. He first intended to make Jews leave the country voluntarily.

Hermann Göring, Hitler's second in command, ran the Gestapo (Geheime Staatspolizei), the dreaded secret police. The Gestapo had powers above the courts. If a court found a defendant not guilty, the Gestapo could still arrest and imprison the individual.

Joseph Göebbels, in charge of propaganda, controlled all media, newspapers, magazines, movies, radio stations and theaters.

Hitler's elite black-shirted personal guard became a political force that symbolized Nazi terrorism and slaughter. Known as the SS, the Schutzstaffel (Protective Squadron) started as a tiny, highly disciplined unit with only 300 members. It began to grow after Hitler placed Heinrich Himmler in charge. By 1930 he had recruited more than 3,000 members, each a "paragon of racial purity."

The SS motto was "Meine Ehre Ist Treue" (Loyalty is my honor). Waffen (military) SS divisions would fight along the Wehrmacht (army), but were answerable only to Hitler. The SS also ran the concentration camps. They wore the Totenkopf (the death's head) as an insignia.

SS duties often overlapped those of the Gestapo. The SS conducted its own door-to-door searches and had its own intelligence unit, the SD (Sicherheitsdienst, or security service), whose duty according to Himmler was to discover "the enemies of the Nazi concept." Reinhard Heydrich was in charge of the SD. He would soon play an important role in Hitler's plan for the Jews, as would Adolf Eichmann, whom Heydrich appointed to head the Department of Jewish Affairs.

The Nazi Party continued to function as a political party. It had branches in every neighborhood and searched for people who were not loyal to Hitler. It organized school children into Hitler youth groups that wore swastika armbands and smartly styled uniforms. They were taught to hate Jews, spy on their parents and report anyone whose loyalty was questionable.

In the fall of 1935, the Nazis pushed through the Reichstag the Nuremberg Racial Laws. A "blood" law stipulated that only persons of "German or German-related blood" could be citizens. Jews became just "subjects" of the German state. The "law for the protection of German blood and German honor" prohibited marriage or sexual relations between Jews and Non-Jews.

Regulations stemming from these laws led to the withdrawal of political rights and to outright persecution of Jews. Using the pretext of Nuremberg law violations, Nazis seized Jewish businesses, authorized the breaking of commercial contracts and the dismissal of Jewish employees. Eventually, Jewish children were barred from attending public schools.

At first, Jews could not comprehend what was happening to them. Jews had lived on German soil since the time of the Roman Empire. Despite savage persecution in medieval times and frequent expulsions from town to town, they had continued over 16 centuries to make important contributions to the development of modern Germany.

In the Weimar Republic, Jews had served in high offices, held important civil service positions and taught in the great universities. Their influence in German intellectual life was great. Of the 38 Nobel prizes won by Germans between 1905 and 1936, 14 were awarded to Jews.

Until Hitler came to power, Germany represented culture and freedom to the European Jewish community. Jews were active in the arts, sciences, literature, industry and the professions.

Jews believed that they had demonstrated their loyalty to Germany during the First World War. More than 100,000 — one in every six Jews of the population — had served in the Kaiser's army, 80 percent in combat roles. Some 12,000 fell in the war and 35,000 were decorated for bravery.

One of the German-Jewish newspapers at that time could read the handwriting on the wall. It warned its readers that the national revolution indicated "that the world of our previous concepts has collapsed." The only survivors would be those who could look reality in the eye.

Jews who looked reality in the eye began to leave Germany. Those who could afford it went to America and other countries out of Hitler's reach. A Jewish welfare agency, the American Joint Distribution Committee (AJDC), helped others go to Palestine.

The remainder could not believe that the madness would continue.

Between 1933 and 1938, the first concentration camps opened in Dachau (near Munich), Sachsenhausen (near Kassel) and Buchenwald (near Weimar). Within one year there would be 50 concentration camps all over Germany.

The practices that were developed in these camps by the SS would become standard in the hundreds of concentration camps that sprung up during the war.

On arrival, prisoners had their heads shaved and identification numbers tattooed on their forearms. They were given jackets and pants made out of cheap striped cloth. Like everything else in camps, these measures were designed to de-humanize inmates.

Critics of the regime were sent to these camps, along with Socialists, Communists, homosexuals, Gypsies and dissident clergymen, as well as Jews. Prisoners were forced to perform back-breaking, sometimes senseless labor for 14 to 16 hours each day. Those who complained or who could not keep up were severely beaten, which led to many deaths. Brutality was the order of the day from the very beginning of the Hitler rule.

As an alternative to the "stick," Hitler offered the "carrot" of propaganda. In *Mein Kampf* (My Battle), he wrote that if propaganda is to be successful, it has to present a simple message to a mass audience. The German people had to believe that they were involved with an "evil" enemy. He placed Göebbels in charge of the Ministry of Public Enlightenment and Propaganda to control the flow of public information through the media.

All newspapers and all other media were controlled by the Ministry of Propaganda, and those who did not follow the official party line or that were owned by Jews were shut down.

Hitler at an S.A. rally celebrating his third anniversary as chancellor. Berlin, Germany, February 20, 1936. USHMM

Hitler at S.A. rally

The theme of all Nazi propaganda was the cult of the Führer, the Great Charismatic Leader. It was designed to create a closeness and folk community bonded to its leader. Allegiance to Hitler was direct, personal and absolute, replacing all other loyalties, be it to family or other bonds.

Germans were constantly told that they were superior to all other races such as the Slavs, Gypsies or blacks. Jews were the worst of all, being on the bottom of all races. But the German people were the "highest species of humans on this earth."

In October 1933, Hitler took Germany out of the League of Nations, the forerunner of the United Nations founded after the First World War. He also pulled out of the Geneva disarmament conference, claiming Germany was not given equality with other nations. This defied the Treaty of Versailles, which ended the First World War, and made it pos-

18

sible for the Germans to re-arm.

In March 1935, Hitler announced that he would rebuild the German Army. In 1936, he sent troops into the demilitarized Rhineland. The Western nations, which had the power to stop Hitler and end the danger right there, did nothing.

With an efficient war machine and his borders secure, Hitler turned to expanding the Third Reich. His first victim was Austria.

The Austro-Hungarian monarchy had been a multi-nation state covering a large part of the European continent, embracing many different peoples who spoke many different dialects and languages. The monarchy had been constantly expanding at the cost of other nations and had occupied many territories.

1830-1916

Emperor Franz Josef I

In 1908, the annexation of Bosnia-Herzegovina led to a crisis in which war with Serbia was averted at the last possible moment. The Russians were too weak to come to Serbia's aid, since they had just lost a war with Japan (1905) and had given up their main port on the Pacific coast, Port Arthur.

On the Austro-Hungarian throne sat Emperor Franz Josef I. Born in 1830, he ascended to govern at the age of eighteen and reigned as emperor of Austria from 1848 to 1916, and as king of Hungary from 1867 to 1916. The heir to the throne, Rudolph von Habsburg, romantically involved with an actress, Mary Vetchera, committed suicide in a hunting lodge in Meyerling, a small town near Vienna.

The next logical choice to follow the emperor upon his death was his nephew, Franz Ferdinand. As closest relative in line for the throne, Ferdinand was hated by the Southern (Yugo) Slavs for wanting to incorporate the South Slavic lands into the monarchy. The Serbs opposed any more

Austrian expansion plans because they saw themselves as the heirs to the territory now under Austrian rule. Their goal was to establish a greater Serbian empire.

In June 1914, Franz Ferdinand and his wife Sophie von Hohenberg were on a good will tour to the South Slavic region when they were assassinated in Sarajevo.

The assassination was one of the defining moments of the 20th Century. One month after Franz Ferdinand's death, the Austro-Hungarian ambassador to Belgrade handed the Serbs an ultimatum "henceforth to resist from all anti-Austrian propaganda," which Serbia rejected.

Russia, meanwhile, declared that "under no circumstances" would it permit aggression against Serbia. The Austrians broke off diplomatic relations with Serbia. Following this Serbia mobilized.

The political situation deteriorated within days. Austria declared war on Serbia on July 28. This prompted Russia's Czar Nicholas II to come to the aid of his fellow Slavs in Serbia. On July 30, Russia began moving troops to the border region. France, as Russia's ally, ordered a general mobilization the following day. Germany rallied to Austria's defense and declared war on Russia. Forty-eight hours later, Berlin declared war on France and sent its troops into Belgium. This forced England, bound by treaty, to defend Belgian neutrality, and prompted anti-Russian Turkey to side with Austria and Germany.

The ensuing Great War cost the lives of 8.6 million combatants and 6.5 million civilians. By the end of 1918, more than a generation of Europe's best lay dead in the trenches. The Austrian Empire was in shambles, the Ottoman Turks had retreated to Anatolia and the last of the Romanovs of Russia lay buried in an Ekaterinburg grave.

Emperor Franz Joseph did not live to see the end of the war: He died in 1916 and his grand-nephew, Karl, ascended to the throne. By the end of the war, he was forced to abdicate and sent into exile, as was Germany's King Wilhelm.

The monarchy fell apart. A new Europe was created out

of the remnants of the old. Austria lost South Tyrol and the corridor to the Adriatic Sea to Italy. Slovenia, Croatia, Bosnia-Herzegovina, Montenegro and Macedonia joined under one flag as Yugoslavia under the undisputed leadership of Serbia with Belgrade as its capital. Bohemia and Moravia joined with Slovakia, Carpato-Ukraine and the Sudetenland to become a united Czechoslovakia. Hungary remained a kingdom without a king and a new Poland was created out of Galicia (South Poland) and former German territories (North Poland) including a corridor to the North Sea, effectively splitting Germany in two.

Austria was reborn as a republic on November 12, 1918. Out of the many nationalities, only one remained. Out of the many countries, only one remained. Out of a population of about 50 million, only about 6 million remained. Out of many resources, only a few remained. This was the immediate picture that emerged and the world did not give too much hope that this truncated, newly created Austrian republic could survive.

The idea of a union with Germany was born, but it was forbidden under the terms of the peace agreement with the Western powers.

The years after the loss of the empire were marked with immense hardships, unemployment and uncontrolled inflation. The economy was in shambles and armed confrontations took place on the southern and eastern borders of the infant state.

To make matters worse, living quarters were in short supply. With the winter of 1918-1919 knocking on the door and no coal available, the situation did not endear the government to the populace.

Furthermore, for the past four war years no new apartment houses were erected in Vienna and many of the existing buildings were in dire need of repair or beyond repair. De-commissioned soldiers and former prisoners of war streamed into the towns and cities of Austria, looking for work and for a roof over their heads, multiplying the already desperate situation.

In this chaotic situation, anti-Semitism raised its ugly head again. Echoes of long-forgotten clichés started to emerge. Jews were being accused of having killed Christ and old blood libel cases were rehashed and brought to the surface.

In the Middle Ages, Jews were not permitted to follow certain trades. The institutions of higher learning were closed to them; in many cities and towns, they were crammed into ghettos and forced to wear a yellow hat or a yellow armband. But by being forced to live in their own environment, they were also forced to maintain their individuality and turning inward, maintained the Jewish faith and the tenets of the Torah.

The jobs open to them were to be tradesmen, peddlers and jewelers or to act as money-lenders, just to name a few.

The ability to read and write and their knowledge and understanding of money lending led to the creation of a banking system and eventually to the owning of banks. Anti-Jewish hatred was kindled even more when these Jewish bankers made loans to the non-Jewish population and had the "nerve" to demand the money back when it came due.

Through the emancipation that started with Napoleon I, Jews were finally free to follow other professions. Although the universities still maintained a "numerus clausus" limiting the number of Jewish students, Jews started to excel in all professions, in science, in literature, in the medical sciences and also became famous writers and philosophers, poets, actors, etc.

Monetary stability in the new Austrian Republic started with the introduction and issuance of new money, the Schilling, but the political situation remained volatile. The country was governed by a coalition of Christian Socialists, Social Democrats and the Nationalist German Party. Early in 1932, Engelbert Dollfuss became chancellor and a dispute in the parliament brought the dismissal of this assembly.

Dollfuss now reigned by edict, supported by the Homefront, an organization supported by the political right. Alarmed at the increasing power of the Nazis, Dollfuss maneuvered to negotiate an accommodation with Hitler. But to accomplish this, he had to meet the demands of his right-wing allies to crush an alleged left-wing insurrection in the working class district of the capital. Both sides had raised and equipped private forces, and the situation on the streets of Vienna had become explosive.

The strike that had been called in February 1934 ended with the defeat of the Social-Democratic forces when government artillery shelled the Karl-Marx Hof and other apartment buildings in the 21st district. Hundreds were killed and wounded in four days of bloody street fighting before the workers' insurrection was ruthlessly crushed and all opposition parties outlawed.

Meanwhile, the Nazis had started their own reign of terror, culminating in a coup d'état in July 1934 with the assassination of Chancellor Dollfuss. The Nazis seized power but only for one day before Kurt von Schusschnig became the Austrian Chancellor.

4. The world I was born into

This is the world I am born into. What do I remember first? Is it my first birthday? Do I remember the cake and the candle, when I was taken out of my crib to join the festivities? Or was it when I was sitting on the kitchen table and crying my eyes out, because I wanted what I had yesterday and nobody could remember that I ate Quargel (Limburger cheese)? Or in the evening lying in bed in the room I shared with my sister, when she told me fairy tales until either one of us fell asleep?

What were my first impressions? Going to public school, where I mastered all subjects easily and my very neat handwriting brought praises from the teacher? Is it that between twenty-some kids in the classroom there were only four Jewish boys and after the first mandatory religious instructions we were accused of having killed their god?

My teacher, Herr Vasicek, kept me after school to talk and gave me pressed Edelweiss as a gift. I would later find out that he was a secret Nazi, although the party was then illegal in Austria.

We had four classes of public school, and after finishing these four years and passing the mandatory exams I was admitted to the Chajes-Real Gymnasium. After my admittance, Herr Vasicek wanted to know why my parents had selected this particular school. I explained to him that this was a Jewish school and my father did not want me to be exposed to anti-Semitism.

The curriculum was very difficult and much was expected from each individual. The daily routine included two hours of Latin, one hour Hebrew, and one hour devoted to the study of the Chumash (the five books of Moses). We also studied English, German, geography, Jewish history and all other subjects usually taught in institutions of higher learning. Unfortunately my first year in this school was frequently interrupted due to throat aches with high temperatures. My studies suffered and I had a hard time keeping up with the curriculum as a mediocre student. The school, being a Jewish institute, was closed on Saturday but open the other six days from 8 a.m. to 3:30 or 4 p.m. This timetable infringed on the normal routine of the family and very little free time remained. Free time was usually spent with family, with the uncles, aunts and cousins we were visiting, or who visited us. In the springtime we ventured into the Vienna woods, where we would picnic and play.

The summer usually took us to the country, where my parents rented an apartment or a house. A number of summers were spent in Vöslau, at a spa near Vienna. The summer of 1937, we vacationed in a small village, just beyond the Semmering mountains, Spital am Semmering, in a villa owned by a Mr. Dedek, who maintained an apiary on the grounds.

While we children lived in a cocoon of safety, the world around us was crumbling. My school was in the twentieth district of the city, about half an hour from our apartment in Mariahilf by trolley car. The school was supported entirely by tuition and was housed in a building owned by the city. In the immediate area of the school was a synagogue, where we children were sometimes taken for special occasions or services. The rabbi, in charge of this house of worship, was a corpulent man with a pig-like fat face, Rabbi Murmelstein.

To instill more patriotism, we had to wear a triangular pin in the colors of the flag of the country: red-white-red, with a green oak leaf in the center and the words "Seid einig" (stay united) engraved upon it. If one forgot or lost the pin, one had to replace it before being permitted to return to the classroom.

Meanwhile the political situation worsened. Italy, which acted as guarantor for Austria's independence, withdrew this guarantee after Italian dictator Mussolini met with Hitler.

In order to avoid a German takeover of Austria, Chancellor Schuschnigg tried to appease the Germans by naming an arch-Nazi to his cabinet. At the same time the Austrians tried to get guarantees from some of the Western powers, but to no avail.

In the beginning of 1938, Hitler summoned Schuschnigg to his retreat at Berchtesgaden. Schuschnigg tried to get Hitler to guarantee Austria's independence if he would name Nazis to certain high positions in the government and pardon Nazis imprisoned for major crimes.

Hitler insisted that the Nazi Party be legalized. He also insisted the chancellor appoint a Nazi interior minister and also fill the position of the finance minister with a known Nazi. If the Austrian did not agree, German troops were ready to cross the border and occupy Austria.

The Austrian chancellor agreed in principle to the Nazi's demands and, hoping to gain time, explained that the constitution required all international agreements to be approved by the Austrian president.

He hoped to use this time to persuade Britain, France and Italy to guarantee Austria's independence. This plea fell on deaf ears.

The president of Austria agreed on February 15, 1938 to back Hitler's demands and instructed Schuschnigg to form a new cabinet with two Nazis in positions of power. Arthur Seyss-Inquart was appointed minister of the interior, effectively controlling the police force, and another Nazi became minister of finance, controlling the economy.

The Nazi Party was legalized and Schuschnigg invited

all political parties to join him and to re-open the parliament. It was too late.

The question of whether Austria should remain independent was to be decided by a national vote on March 13, 1938.

Walking one evening on one of the better-known shopping streets (Mariahilferstrasse) with my mother and sister, we encountered a number of demonstrations and counter-demonstrators, with the Nazis confronting the Fatherland. Police stood by and watched the fights without raising a finger.

Leaflets were tossed from rooftops, littering the streets and sidewalks.

My mother's remarks still ring in my ear, as she said: "Children, look at this carefully. This means war."

The propaganda heated up the closer we came to the plebiscite. The Fatherland Front (Christian Socialists) seemed to hold the edge. Their slogans were painted on the sidewalks and their leaflets and posters covered the city.

The campaign came to an abrupt end on Friday, March 11.

A special broadcast on the RAVAG radio network interrupted the evening's program. It was 7:50 p.m. when Chancellor Schuschnigg went on the air.

"Today we were driven into an insurmountable situation. The government of the German Reich delivered to us an ultimatum, wherein it was demanded that the president of Austria name a person acceptable to the German government as chancellor. In case we do not agree to these demands, German troops, which are massed on our borders, will march into Austria and break all resistance. The president of Austria ordered me to tell the Austrian people that we surrender in the face of brute force. We have also instructed our armed forces not to resist. God protect Austria."

Our apartment was on the highest floor of the building and it opened to the Southern part of the city. I was standing at the window, suddenly freezing and shaking, looking out over the city, tears running down my face. I thought that this is not possible. It must be a nightmare. I will wake up any moment and it will be all over. But it was neither a dream nor a nightmare, it was cold hard fact. I was hoping against hope that the people will rise as one and declare their loyalty to Austria — Austria for the Austrians, Red White Red unto death (Rot-Weiss-Rot bis in den Tod) — but nothing like this happened. This was the most horrible, blackest day of my life until then.

Seyss-Inquart was appointed chancellor, while German troops occupied Austria, receiving a jubilant welcome from the population. Two days later, Anschluss — the union of Austria with Germany — was announced by Hitler.

Walking out on the street the next morning, I was astounded to find the city bedecked with swastikas, the Nazi flags. I could not stop to wonder where all these flags had suddenly come from. Storm troopers in their brown uniforms complete with swastika armbands were patrolling the streets.

For Austrian Jews, Anschluss meant disaster. In the following months, the Nazis totally excluded the Jews, setting the pattern to be followed in other, later occupied lands. Austria had a long tradition of anti-Semitism and many Austrian politicians set out to prove that they disliked the Jews as much as the Nazis did.

5. The terror begins

When the Germans came, there were 185,000 Jews in Austria, most of them living in Vienna. Suddenly Jews were attacked on the streets. The beards of Orthodox Jews were forcefully shaved. Crowds jeered while Jewish women, including my mother, were compelled to scrub the sidewalks free of the election slogans painted onto the sidewalks by the Fatherland Front. Order of some sort was restored, but anti-Semitism continued in more sinister forms.

Jews washing the streets in Vienna

The SS established the Central Office for Jewish Emigration, a passport office under the direction of Adolf Eichmann, the German-born, Austrian-raised "Jewish specialist." It was housed in a mansion confiscated from Baron Louis de Rothschild.

In order to obtain a passport, each individual had to report to the Palais, as it was commonly called. The Palais was surrounded by a high wall, with the caretaker's hut and a single door at the end of the estate. This was the door through which Jews were allowed to enter. Before I had a chance to walk through this door, I witnessed an elderly, well-dressed Jewish gentleman knock on the door and doff his hat, saying "good morning" to the guard. He opened the door, walked in, turned around and proceeded going in and out over and over again. The guard screamed and ordered him to repeat it until he learned how to greet him properly. I don't remember what procedure we had to follow in order to obtain our passports, but I remember the most impressive layout of Rothschild's palace, with a mirrored hall equal in beauty to Versailles, made unclean by the presence of many Nazis including Eichmann walking around, barking orders.

Adolf Eichmann

Finally we were issued our passports, with a large red "J" on the first page. We were forced to add "Israel" and the women "Sara" as middle names. The "J" in the passports was by request of the Swiss government, which wanted to make sure Switzerland would not be overrun by German Jewish refugees. (Refugees apprehended by the Swiss were turned back and arrested by the Germans, only to wind up in a concentration camp).

Every day brought new laws and new restrictions for the Jewish population. Many Jewish businesses were closed and transferred to non-Jewish ownership. Sixty percent of all Jewish apartments and homes were taken over for "Aryan" use.

Schools were closed for the time being, which afforded us children an extended holiday, not realizing what all this would lead to.

My father's business was not touched at that time because two partners, Uncle Leo and Uncle Isidor, were Polish citizens. Although on the first Sunday following the occupation of Austria, Uncle Leo was taken by the S.A., driven to the business and forced to donate a truckload of loden coats.

Palais Rothschild

Jews were dismissed from government and other public employment. They were forbidden to work as lawyers, and Jewish doctors could serve only the Jewish populace. Jewish writers were not allowed to publish their works. Jewish newspapers were closed and all books written by Jews were burned. Heinrich Heine (1797-1856) the famous German-Jewish writer, said in his days: "Where one burns books, one will, in the end burn people."

Jews pushed out of public life found themselves marooned in the middle of nowhere.

To make the occupation of Austria legal, Hitler ordered a plebiscite for April 10, 1938. The result: 99% of the population voted "yes" to the Anschluss. With the union now legalized, Austria ceased to exist. The country's name disappeared from the maps, the name "Ostmark" (Eastern bulwark) was substituted. Austrian lands, like states in America, were renamed to the German Gau. The capital, Vienna, the former seat of the Austro-Hungarian empire, the city that had been the cultural and industrial center of

Europe, turned into a second- rate provincial town.

Anti-Jewish measures seemed to be the priority of the government. One chased the next. Jews had to surrender all valuables. Jews were not permitted to own gold, and there was a limit on how many silver objects Jews could keep. Radios had to be turned in to the local police station and the remaining Jewish businesses had to display the name of their company in Yiddish letters.

The schools were re-opened in September, but all Jewish students in regular schools were dismissed.

Toward the middle of October 1938, Poland, which also had a long history of anti-Semitism, ruled that all Polish citizens not on the territory of the Polish republic at a certain date in October would forfeit their citizenship.

Herschel Grynszpan

The Germans acted swiftly and arrested all male bearers of Polish passports. My father's partners, Uncle Leo and Uncle Isidor, were arrested along with Uncle Meyer (Dressler). Leo and Isidor were among the many taken to the Polish border and pushed across. Uncle Meyer died in police custody.

Both surviving uncles chose to settle in Lwow (formerly Lemberg) and made arrangements for their families to follow.

On November 6, 1938, a young Jewish man, Herschel Grynszpan, whose father had also been shipped across the Polish border, walked into the German embassy in Paris and shot Third Secretary Vom Rath. He set out to kill the German ambassador but could not find him, so he killed the first official that he came in contact with.

This matter was just the excuse the Nazis had been waiting for. They ordered a pogrom against the Jewish population of Germany.

My father's place of business, bombed in 1943

It started on the night of November 9th and ended 24 hours later. All synagogues in the Reich were dynamited or burned to the ground. All Jewish businesses were "sealed," confiscated without compensation and taken over by non-Jews. Mass arrests ensued and all men arrested were sent to the Dachau or Buchenwald concentration camps.

For all the "damages done to the Reich property" by Nazi storm troopers, SS and Hitler Youths, Göring in his devilish design, ordered that the Jewish population be assessed to pay a fine of 1 billion German marks.

My father's business was in the rear of an apartment house in the second district of the city, Leopoldsstadt, Obere Donaustraße 35. It was not a business with a storefront, as it was a wholesale place. It occupied the entire first floor of this building, with a later added-on wing that contained the cutting rooms and served as auxiliary storage facility. Across the garden was the dress department with a long narrow building containing perhaps 40 to 50 sewing machines, manned by as many women, busy making garments.

In the main part of the business there were different departments, like women's and men's coats, suits, fur coats, children's outerwear, raincoats and bookkeeping offices. The head bookkeeper was a Mr. Jaeger assisted by Miss Schwartz. The cutting room was run by a Mr. Ballogg, who was originally from Bohemia, where all the good tailors had come from.

On the second floor of this building, we had the unpleasant experience of having to put up with the local chapter of the Nazi Party.

I was at school as usual on this fateful day. We had just returned from the gym, with the next subject being history. Professor Kofler, who taught history, as well as geography, was pacing up and down the classroom. Finally he told us what was happening and said he would have no objection if anybody wanted to leave.

Destroyed main synagogue, Vienna

I was called to the office, where Mr. Ballogg was waiting for me. He escorted me to my father's business, a walk of about twenty minutes. On route we passed a number of trucks loaded with storm troopers screaming anti-Semitic slogans.

As soon as I arrived, the telephone rang. My Aunt Mollie told my father to take a cab to her place, since "they" had been there already and had searched her apartment (although she was a Polish citizen).

Herr Ballogg had gotten us a cab. As the driver started to pull away from the curb, a brown-shirted S.A. man tried unsuccessfully to rip open the door.

As the cab passed through the first district, I saw the rioters had set fire to the main synagogue in Vienna and mobs were marching through the streets.

Kurzgasse 3

I dropped my father off at my aunt's place in the Köstlergasse and continued on to our apartment in the Kurzgasse. Four Jewish families lived in this apartment house of about 22 tenants. There were our immediate neighbors, Mr. and Mrs. Taskier, whose daughter Annie had recently gotten married and moved to France. There was Mama and her son Heinzie Gross, who eventually emigrated to the Dominican Republic, and there was Dr. and Mrs. Freudenthal. Dr. Freudenthal must have had Alzheimer's disease; he had misdiagnosed me years earlier when I had a childhood disease. There was another Jewish family whose name I cannot remember, but right across the courtyard, seemingly close enough to touch, lived Mrs. Kelbig. She was Jewish, her husband was not.

Mrs. Kelbig was the central office for gossip. She knew everything that went on within five kilometers and broadcast the news from window to window across the courtyard. Mr. Kelbig was a permanent optimist. He was certain this "Hitler thing" could not last long. "In a few weeks, if not days, it will be all over."

On the floor below us was a dentist's office: Dr. Adolph Schnoflack and his son by the same name. He had been an illegal Nazi, and his son paraded in the S.A. uniform from day one.

When I reached home, I found my mother very upset, not knowing what the next few hours would bring. The S.A. and the Nazi Party members were looting Jewish apartments and arresting most of the men for shipment to the concentration camps.

Unknown to us at that time was that young Schnoflack, who was involved in looting other apartments, would not let anything happen to "his" Jews and held watch in front of our apartment house.

After 24 hours, quiet descended on the city. All the synagogues were in ashes, the burned parchment of the torahs mingling with the dust. All Jewish businesses were taken, glass littering the streets and thousands of Jews suffering and dying in concentration camps.

Boycott

My father's business was sealed. Upon intervention by the Polish embassy, the business was permitted to re-open a week or two later. But my father had to liquidate by December 31, 1938 and turn the key and all furniture over to the Nazi Party, which would now occupy the first floor. My father was forced to sell the stock for five cents on the dollar, or perhaps for less.

In later readings, I found out that the Hitler hordes wanted to test the reaction to this type of excess against the Jews. Since no one anywhere in the world objected, the Nazis felt very secure in pursuing their anti-Jewish programs.

Toward the end of November, both the Epsteins and the Glanzmanns moved to Poland. Their belongings were packed into big moving vans and shipped to Lwow, where the women's husbands awaited them.

On the moving day, Aunt Regina called and told my parents that the customs inspector was a nice guy. If they brought the valuables to her place, she would smuggle them out under the eyes of the customs man. In retrospect it is ludicrous to think that saving some valuables would be the most important thing to do — but who knew what was to come? My parents took jewelry, fur coats, the sterling cutlery, my father's stamp collection and some other silver objects to my aunt. She succeeded in packing it in and shipping it out.

My father had been an ardent Zionist all his life. He donated to the Keren Kayemet and the Keren Hayessod and was entered in the Golden book of both organizations. Having been a big donator to Zionist causes, he had applied for a certificate that would enable us to emigrate to Palestine.

For his services to the British Crown during the First World War, Chaim Weitzman, a chemist living in London, was to be honored with the highest British award. He declined in favor of a promise by the British government to establish a Jewish homeland in the territory of Palestine, which was taken in warfare from the Turks.

In 1917, Lord Balfour, the British foreign minister, issued the so-called "Balfour Declaration" in which "His Majesty's government guarantees the establishment of a Jewish homeland in Palestine." The Arabs protested vehemently. Privately, the British also guaranteed the Arabs a homeland in the same territory. The British MI6 was actively involved in trying to split the Zionist movement and to "create an opposition in relation to Zionism and Dr. Weitzman."

(This was revealed in the MI6 secret report of master spy Burgess to the NKVD Soviet secret police as recounted in Deadly Illusions by Oleg Tsarev.)

Eventually the British government issued a White Paper limiting Jewish immigration to a trickle. I believe it was about 1,500 people a year.

My family's quest to join them began with an application for immigration through a quasi-embassy in Vienna known as the Palestine Office.

My father had befriended a Mr. Niedermayer, who was in the shipping business. Niedermayer had emigrated to Palestine, and through his connections and the help of Moshe Smilansky, a deposit of one thousand British pounds was made in my father's name in the British Bank of Palestine.

Mr. Niedermayer informed us that everything was in order and we should ship all our belongings into his care to Haifa.

My parents contracted with a company called Caro & Jellinek to ship everything, including the furniture, in a three-meter lift. A lift was a container made out of wood that was not to be returned.

On the given day, a crew came with this monster lift and loaded it to capacity. The customs inspector confiscated four little silver spoons that in his opinion were too heavy and could not be exported.

A few days later we were informed that because we tried to export silver, which was on the list of forbidden items, the whole lift was confiscated. After many days of running about, this judgment was reversed. The lift could start its journey to Haifa, but we never would.

The destination was denied to us through circumstances of greed, corruption and war.

Mr. Niedermayer insisted that the certificate had been issued and my father should check with the Palestine office in Vienna. He went to see a Mr. Bartfeld, the man in charge, who kept insisting that the certificate was not issued and he would be the only one to know. Later we found out Bartfeld had sold our certificate to the highest bidder for 66,000 German Marks, then the equivalent of one thousand English pounds.

Bartfeld was a fat man who suddenly started losing weight. He and his family escaped to Italy with all the money he must have amassed, but he died soon after his arrival.

We were left with only a handful of things we were not planning to take with us: A few cots to sleep on, the kitchen table and other odds and ends that suddenly attained major importance.

Mr. Niedermayer confirmed the arrival of the lift in Haifa. It was later sold at auction, since there was no money to pay for storage.

Kinder Transport

Jews tried to emigrate, but most countries had closed their doors to them. The lines around the American embassy to register for immigration to the United States stretched around the block. Under the quota system, one could expect to wait four to six years. Other countries denied visas to holders of German passports marked with the red "J."

Great Britain permitted children to immigrate in so-called Kinder Transporte, children's transports. Mothers and fathers had only a few days to fill a single suitcase with clothing and family keepsakes for the long journey that their children would be making alone. There seemed even less time to cram into the child's head and heart with family attachments and feelings they had assumed would take a lifetime to teach.

Yet in 1938 and '39, that was the agonizing task facing Jewish parents in Germany, Austria and Czechoslovakia who signed their children up for this massive humanitarian effort overseen by the British and consented to by the Nazis that allowed 10,000 kids to flee their homelands (and the coming Holocaust) by boarding trains bound for England and waiting foster families.

Every parent promised their child that they would soon

follow. It was a promise very few would be able to keep.

In order to defy the British and create discord between the Jewish and Arab population in Palestine, the Gestapo permitted the Jews to organize "illegal" transports from Germany to Palestine. The Jewish organizations had to provide rail transport and purchase mostly old and shaky ships. Then they had to somehow avoid British patrol boats blockading the coast and land on Palestine soil.

Many of these transports were intercepted on high seas by the British and the people were interned on the island of Cyprus, then a British colony. Also, many were held up by local authorities and had to pay ransom to be released.

My father had equipped and financed the "illegal" emigration of Siggie and Dolphi Dressler. Both young men had left Vienna only to turn up a couple of weeks later in the city. They had not been able to cross the border into Italy or Yugoslavia. After the second try, they were successful and after many days at sea and running the British blockade they landed safely on Palestine soil and were able to spend the war years in the Holy Land.

Siggie was a Socialist and spent most of his time in the surroundings of his party and party colleagues. I was told that he had to escape over the rooftops to safety during the riots of 1934 when the Christian-Socialists fired into the workers homes and Socialist Party headquarters.

Dolphi, on the other hand, was always industrious; he worked for a distant relative, Matjek Kogan, as a dental assistant.

The Dresslers lived in the fifteenth district on the Hütteldorferstrasse, in a one-bedroom apartment. My aunt, Tante Frieda, had a store adjoining the apartment, which my father always stocked with merchandise. To my knowledge, he was never compensated for it. Once a week, Aunt Frieda would come to the house to get money, as would my father's older sister, Anna.

My father also helped his other sister's children, Renia and Nolo Katz, in equipping them and financing their journey by "illegal" transport to Palestine.

Toward the end of 1938, Hitler had forced the Western powers to cede parts of Czechoslovakia to him, namely the territory of the Sudetenland, which was settled mainly by a German-speaking population. In March 1939, Hitler marched into the rest of Czechoslovakia, occupying Moravia and Bohemia and creating Slovakia as a satellite nation. Hitler insisted he had no more territorial demands on any European country, and the Western powers started to relax.

The former bookkeeper, Mr. Jäger, had been arrested in the anti-Jewish pogrom in November 1938 and was sent to the Dachau concentration camp. Upon his release from the camp, he came to visit my father and demanded severance pay; otherwise, he would report father to the authorities. I never found out why my father yielded to his blackmail and paid him off.

With nothing productive to do, my father and I would spend days sitting on the park bench meeting other Jewish men. Then one day the park benches were painted over with the words "For Aryans Only." Soon after, we were forced to take another couple into our apartment, a Mr. and Mrs. Jekel. He was involved in the black market trade and could get anything for anybody.

My mother, always looking out to better my education, registered me into an additional special Hebrew language course that I attended a couple of afternoons weekly. Seated next to me was an elderly gentleman who had lost his left arm fighting in the Kaiser's army as an officer in the First World War. I helped Mr. Kohn many times in explaining to him words or sentences during these Hebrew lessons.

I still attended the Chajes-Real Gymnasium and had regular school hours even though the school was now housed in much smaller quarters in the Castellezgasse. The building they had occupied earlier in the 20th district, Staudingergasse 6, was a public school building rented from the city, which abrogated the lease.

The political situation had again taken a turn for the worse and every day brought reports of skirmishes on the German-Polish border.

The British and the French had dispatched a delegation to the Soviet Union to foster an agreement between the Western powers and the Soviet Union to assure the independence and the territorial integrity of Poland. Negotiations dragged on throughout the summer.

Toward the end of August, the world was shocked to learn that arch-enemies Nazi Germany and Communist Soviet Russia had signed a non-aggression pact. Unknown to the rest of the world, a clause would give each of the signers of this infamous deed "a sphere of influence" in the territory of Poland.

Hitler had played a trump card again, and the way to the East now lay open. Now he could move on Poland without interference from Stalin's Russia.

In this decisive week, suddenly and without warning, ration cards were issued to the population. The superintendent of the building handed us our ration cards, which were marked with a big red "J." Coupons for such items as eggs, butter and jam were crossed out and were not to be used by Jews.

A black-out was ordered immediately. During the night, we heard the rumble of tanks and heavy equipment rattling through the streets of the city.

Hitler called the Reichstag into session on Saturday, Sept. 1, 1939. He declared, that the "Poles had fired on defenseless German women and children, had crossed the border and attacked the German radio station in Gleiwitz (a German border town)." He continued, "since 5:30 this morning we are returning the fire."

As the German Army crossed into Poland, Britain and France issued an ultimatum that Germany withdraw immediately. Treaty-bound as guarantors of Poland, they declared war on Germany on September 3, 1939.

The mightiest army in Europe — or for that matter, in

the world — moved into Poland in a form of warfare never seen before. Blitzkrieg (lightning war) crushed the defenders in a few days and bombed Warsaw into submission. By the 17th of September, Soviet forces started to occupy Poland from the East. Before the month was over, Poland was conquered, divided and had ceased to exist.

Poland before the war was home to three million Jews. About two million of these Polish Jews found themselves now in the territory occupied by the Nazis. Almost immediately, the Germans started to herd these people into ghettos and subject them to forced labor.

As soon as the occupation of Poland was complete, the Jewish Community Council (Israelitische Kultusgemeinde) under order from the Gestapo, sent "invitations" to selected Jewish men, including my father, to report with hand luggage to the burned-out shell of the main synagogue (Seitenstättengasse) in Vienna for the purpose of resettlement and rebuilding the former Polish territories.

During his service in the First World War, father had been injured on the Rumanian front and given status as a 25% invalid. Since he had no intention of reporting for resettlement, I accompanied my mother to plead his case in front of the commission and, based on his war injury, have his name removed from the list. We walked into the sanctuary of the once-magnificent synagogue to find the interior destroyed, the beautiful chandeliers gone, the floor carted away and replaced with sand, and the pews missing. On the bema, where the Holy Ark stood with all the torahs inside, was now nothing but burnt timber.

Now on this bema stood a long table with the commission seated on one side and the candidates lined up in front. I was pleasantly surprised when I recognized Mr. Kohn, my friend from the Hebrew language course, sitting on the selection committee. As soon as I introduced my mother, he tore up my father's "invitation" and removed his name from the list.

Toward the end of 1939, a curfew went into effect, forbid-

43

ding Jews to be on the streets after 4:30 p.m.. My school-days lasted till 4 p.m. and the walk home took at least one hour, forcing me to break the curfew every day. One day I was followed by three Hitler youths, who after calling me names finally caught up with me in front of the barber shop around the corner from my home. They started to beat me and shoved my head so deep into a snow bank that I could hardly breathe. I called for help to Mr. Hrnilicka, the barber who had cut my hair from the time I was a baby. He came out of his store but did not make the slightest effort to come to my aid. After a while, the thugs let me go. Mr. Hrnilicka apologized for his "inaction," but things could never be the same again.

I must admit that with very few exceptions, I had no problems with the boys I'd gone to public school with. Even those in Hitler Youth uniforms would stop to greet me when we met in the street, and we would have friendly conversations.

Early in 1940 we received notice that we had to turn over the key to the apartment to new tenants. We were very lucky to find a large room to sublet on the Linke Wienzeile 4, in the same building where my sister Mary had previously gone to a private school.

Even though Germany was at war with England, it was in Germany's interest that the illegal transports to Palestine continue in order to destabilize the precarious Arab-Jewish balance. Every transport leaving Germany had to find safe or different routes through unfriendly territory, bribing officials in order to get permits of transit and ultimately run the British blockade on high seas. The younger men and women among those lucky enough to reach the shores of the future state of Israel were immediately issued rifles and assigned to watchtowers to defend the Jewish settlements from Arab marauders.

Those not so lucky in reaching the Promised Land were, as I noted before, stopped on the high seas by the British Navy and in most cases interned for the duration of the war on the island of Cyprus.

It brings to mind the case of the Patria, the ship that "blew itself up" in the harbor of Haifa when the British denied the people permission to land and threatened them with expulsion and internment on the island of Madagascar.

The Zionist Youth organizations were still permitted to function in Vienna, and all political factions, from the very left to the very right were housed in a building (Marc-Aurel Strasse 5) hardly one block away from Gestapo headquarters, located in the former Hotel Metropole on the infamous Morzin Platz.

My sister Mary

The leader of the Zionist Youth (Ju-Al, Youth Alia, Jugend Alia), embracing all factions, was Aaron Menczer, a *shaliach* (ambassador) sent by the underground Jewish government of Palestine to organize the Jewish youth movement in Vienna. Aaron came from Dagania Aleph, one of the earliest pioneer settlements in the Jezreel Valley of Israel.

My father had found out that the Zionist youth movement was contemplating sending an illegal transport to the Holy Land. After lengthy discussions, my parents decided it would be the best if my sister could go along.

Father went to see Aaron Menczer. Explaining that he was a Zionist of long standing, he wanted a place for his daughter on the next transport. Aaron explained that there were certain prerequisites, such as being active in the Zionist Youth movement or having served on an experimental agricultural station that the Zionist Youth Movement maintained outside Vienna. Father started to throw his weight around until finally Aaron seemed to agree to his demands.

My sister's bags were packed and she was ready to go, waiting for the call that never came. Aaron Menczer had hidden her passport.

As it turned out, this group left Vienna on a ship floating down the Danube and arrived in Yugoslavia just as the Germans waged war against that country. The young passengers were interned and never heard from again.

My sister and I, however, discovered the Zionist Youth center on Marc Aurel Street, which became our second home. Both of us started to become active and rose in the ranks of the Youth movement.

Toward the middle of 1940, the Germans occupied Denmark and Norway. After out-maneuvering Belgium and the Netherlands, Germany forced France to capitulate. With all these victories, the war situation seemed hopeless. The few who tried to escape now were turned over to the Gestapo and wound up in concentration camps.

Belonging to the Zionist Youth rewarded us with a sense of security in a circle of young people, all in the same situation and allotted us time to be "free" within our own environment.

We made a lot of new friends we would meet in discussions, learning from recognized instructors and professors who had lost their jobs because they were Jews. We spent our leisure time together with song and dance, which later became the song and dance of Israel.

We forged friendships that were supposed to have lasted a lifetime — but then, what was a lifetime? The names that come to mind are mentioned here for a reason. They represent some of the young people whose lives were cut short by the murdering Nazis and who, unfortunately, have become nothing but statistics. Their graves are not adorned by markers or gravestones, for they lie in nameless graves in far-off forests and lonely fields, their ashes scattered by the winds to the four corners of the earth without a trace that they ever existed.

Here, only a few are mentioned, to give them identity and eternity:

There was Aaron Menczer, who, with a group of youngsters, marched into the gas chambers of Auschwitz. There was Kiki (Hans) and Miri (Miriam) Newman, Paul Adler and Trudy Wald, who died together in the ghetto of Minsk. Natzi (Ignatz) Hasterlick, Beppo Loeffler, Waldi (Walter) Klug, Gertie Krieger, Peter Stiasny, Heinzie (Henry) Baer, Georg Strakosch, Rosie Weinstein and many, many more whose names I no longer remember. We take them into our hearts and give them a place beside the cherished memories of our own loved ones. They are now ours.

As Jews, our participation in public life by now had virtually ceased. We were not permitted to go to movie houses or theaters. Many shopkeepers had signs in their windows: "Jews Not Wanted," "Jews Not Permitted," or "No Jews-No Dogs." Or simply "Jews Forbidden."

We came to appreciate our little world and spent more time together. As an organization we planned many events. We had our own theater production, we organized an exhibit of our own handicrafts and made secret excursions into the Vienna woods, which were now forbidden to Jews.

To supply the Jewish hospital and Jewish old-age home, the Jewish Community Center maintained two vegetable gardens where we spent many afternoons working the land. One was on the unused portion of the Jewish cemetery and the other one in one of the outlying districts of the city.

The Zionist group I belonged to was "The Betar," on the right side of the political spectrum. The Betar believed, as was later proven correct, that a Jewish state could only be created with armed might. Our program included paramilitary training in preparation for the mission we hoped would fulfill our ideas and ideals.

Europe had collapsed under the Nazi onslaught. On April 9, 1940 Hitler invaded Denmark and Norway, subduing them in a matter of days. On May 10, German armies swept through the Low Countries: Belgium, the Netherlands and Luxemburg. The Netherlands fell in five days, Belgium in three weeks. A British army was trapped and had to be evacuated from the beaches of Dunkirk.

The demoralized French Army offered little resistance to Hitler's tank divisions. Paris fell on June 13, 1940. An armistice divided France in two parts, The North was occupied by the Germans and parts of the Southeast were occupied by Mussolini's Italy, which had entered the war days before the armistice.

The rest of France came under control of the Vichy government headed by Marshal Petain, the French hero of World War I. Vichy was really a puppet of Germany. After the war, Petain was found guilty of collaborating with the enemy and sentenced to death although he was never executed.

The next step Hitler planned was the invasion of England. In preparation, the Luftwaffe launched massive bombing raids but the Royal Air Force offered unexpectedly stiff resistance. Between July and October, the Germans lost 1,722 aircraft, while the RAF's losses stood at 915. The invasion was called off.

With England out of reach, Hitler began to prepare for Operation Barbarossa, code name for the invasion of the Soviet Union. In April 1941, with Bulgaria and Rumania already under German domination, Hitler invaded Greece and Yugoslavia. Both countries proved difficult to subdue, forcing Germany to postpone the invasion of Russia until the end of June and, subsequently, to fight in the deadly Russian winter.

There were no immediate changes in our little world. We met in our building, pursuing our interests and burying our heads in the sand. Our leaders, Kiki and Paul, suggested and we agreed to conduct a "rabbit hunt" in the Vienna woods. At a given time and place, Kiki and Paul would leave a trail of paper or stones and we, 26 boys, were to follow this trail to find them.

We met to start the hunt but could not find any trace of the markings that Kiki and Paul allegedly had left behind.

As we were standing at a crossroad in the woods, discussing which way to proceed, suddenly and without warning we were surrounded by a police detachment threatening us with drawn weapons. Their leader, screaming and yelling, gesticulating like a contortionist, declared that we were under arrest and we would be shot.

Lined up two by two, we were marched into the police station and ordered to stand with our faces against the wall. After half an hour or perhaps longer, each of us was called inside the station house, searched and interrogated.

Facing the wall, I slowly turned my knapsack to the front and removed an orange. This orange was bought in the black market and it was a dead give-away. It was not obtainable for Jew or non-Jew, and it would have invited lots of questions. First I squeezed it dry, and then I dropped the orange, torn in little pieces into the sand or gravel to my feet and was able to cover the evidence. I was not so lucky with the five-inch Turkish dagger that I carried. The police, off course, confiscated my prized possession.

We were released and instructed to report to our Youth organization headquarters. Aaron Menczer was summoned to the Gestapo. The news he returned with hit us like a ton of bricks. Our school and meeting place, our Youth-Alija, would be closed "forthwith" and we had a choice of either reporting to a labor camp in Doppeln, near Vienna, or else seek employment in or near the city.

I went to the unemployment office and was sent to Terranova Industries, a company engaged in manufacturing mortar mixes and camouflage paints. The place of employment was about half an hour by train south of the city, in the village of Neu Erlaa, which was developed like an industrial center, with many different factories and warehouses.

The work in the plant consisted of crushing and dousing limestone rocks, drying sand and creating a mixture of sand, limestone (which now had become a fine powdery substance), cement and some coloring agent. We then filled this mixture into 50-kilo (about 100-pound) bags for shipment.

I started working on the mixing machine, filling the drums that held up to 2,000 kilos at one time. At other times I worked the sand dryer or crushed the limestone rocks with a sledge hammer.

My friend Natzi Hasterlick had been sent by the unemployment office to sort garbage at the dump. He got a release from that job by claiming illness and came to work at Terranova. Soon afterward, Georg Strakosch and Peter Stiasny joined our ranks.

On June 22, 1941 Hitler invaded the Soviet Union. Three million German troops attacked on a front stretching from the White to the Black Sea.

Hitler insisted that the invasion was necessary "to secure for the German people the land and the spoils to which they are entitled to on this earth. ...Only thus we should gain the Lebensraum (living space) which we need...."

Stalin, who had mistrusted everyone, was constantly afraid of being removed from power by force. In the 1930's, he purged his general staff and removed most of his trained officers. Yet of all people, he had trusted Hitler. When he was informed of the German build-up of three million men, he waved it away with a gesture of his hand.

When the Germans attacked, they faced inexperienced officers and men ill-prepared and equipped with outdated and outmoded arms.

The conquest of the Soviet Union progressed rapidly. By mid-September 1941, Panzer divisions captured Kiev, the country's third-largest city, then pulled out and rolled toward Moscow. Hitler made sure his commanders understood that this conflict was not merely between states, but a battle to the finish between two opposing world views. The "Jewish-Bolshevik" intelligentsia was as much an enemy as the Red army. All Jews were members of this conspiracy;

all Jews would have to be annihilated. The Jews would be the responsibility of the SS, which would follow the army into the Soviet Union and assume control of conquered territories and their inhabitants. In a departure from usual (German) military procedure, a force of SS would actually accompany the invading army. Small mobile units called Einsatzgruppen would rid the freshly taken territories of their undesirable civilian elements, meaning the Jews.

On September 19, 1941, a law went into effect requiring Jews to wear the Jewish star, a black Magen David on yellow fabric with the word "Jude" in mock Hebrew letters upon it. The law stipulated that the star had to be securely fastened to the left side of the outer garment and that it must be visible and cannot be obstructed or covered up.

We found ourselves thrown back into the Middle Ages, when Jews had to wear yellow hats and were forced to live in ghettos.

Laws to segregate the Jewish populations had already taken effect in the occupied territories of Poland and the Soviet Union. Ghettos had been created, and Jews in the Polish territories had already been forced to wear a white armband with a six-pointed Star of David. In the former Polish lands ceded to the Soviet Union in 1939, Jews had to wear a star cut out of a yellow fabric sewn onto the right front and right back. Jews in the occupied regions of the Soviet Union wore a three-inch round, yellow patch on their right front and back.

Wearing the yellow star was another step created to demean the Jews and make it easier for the anti-Semites to identify, harass and discriminate against this "enemy" of the German people.

I had grown out of all my things, and even after using some of my father's garments I was forced to go out and buy clothing in the black market. Everything else we owned had wound up in Palestine.

I walked through the street wearing black-market boots, a loden coat and a hat pulled deep in my face. A zippered briefcase under my left arm covered the star. When I came close to the house we lived in, I turned the left corner and in doing so slid the briefcase off and exposed the star.

My friends and I also frequented movie houses, but always selecting seats near the emergency exits in case of a raid.

One time I walked into a sportswear clothing store and selected a windbreaker. The lady behind the counter asked me for my clothing coupons, which were needed to purchase garments, fabrics or shoes and that were not issued to Jews. I told her I did not have any coupons, but that I have "this" — and with that, I slid my briefcase off my yellow star. Without blinking an eye she accepted my money, thanked me very much for visiting her store and hoped I would come again.

While we young men could seek employment in the vicinity instead of being sent to a labor camp, the girls of our Zionist Youth group had no choice. They were sent, under the leadership of my sister Mary to a camp near Berlin, Stendahl.

There they had to labor at a literally back-breaking job, cutting asparagus from early morning until late night.

Transports of Jews throughout the Reich to the Eastern territories had been dormant for some time, but now they resumed. This time whole families were being arrested and shipped east to destinations unknown.

My sister's group was sentenced to work in this camp apparently forever. The only ones released were the ones whose parents had been arrested to be shipped East and were permitted to wait until their daughters could join up with them.

When one of the girls came down with diphtheria and the camp had to be quarantined, the asparagus growers realized that they had lost their cheap labor force. They insisted that the girls be shipped back to Vienna. Arriving in Vienna, they were not allowed to debark and were held for three more days in the railcar, which was pushed onto an unused siding in the Western rail station. After that the Department of Health lifted the quarantine and the girls were released.

My friends and I would spend Sunday mornings in a bath house in the inner city. It was a place to meet, discuss events, swim and shower — and we would be treated to a good meal in the cafeteria. (Where the owner of the cafeteria got the food from will always remain an enigma). We also would visit St. Stephens' Cathedral to listen to the sermon of Archbishop Innitzer addressing "the children of God, who have no houses of worship." He and the other Roman Catholic clergy had originally supported the Anschluss of Austria to Germany, but this love affair had not lasted too long. A turn-about in the Roman Catholic position results in punitive measures including the sacking and the destruction of the archbishop's palace by the Nazis, which I witnessed.

In late fall, the production at Terranova came practically to a standstill. We still had to crush rocks and prepare sand for the coming season, but my time was taken up by new duties. The foreman in charge, Mr. Hirsch, took me under his wings and I had to help repair machinery and equipment, thereby learning the ins and outs of carpentry and the workings of a blacksmith.

Unfortunately my duties also included making fire in the office and workshop stoves. No matter what I did, I could not get the fire started. Looking for a solution, I discovered a large room, upstairs near the office that was prepared to house prisoners of war, who would eventually be detailed to work in this plant. The floor of this room was heaven-sent. It was neatly laid out with wooden, tar-covered bricks

— just what the doctor ordered. With one brick chopped into little pieces, I could start the fire in the workshop as well as in the office with one match. But soon my misdeed was discovered. I was called on the carpet and bawled out in the third person, as "What did he do?" I had to admit to my obvious sin, and from that time on I had a hard time starting that damned fire.

By then, we were about 20 Jewish people working in this plant. We were treated politely and respected as equals by the administration and the rest of the workers with the exception of one anti-Semitic lab technician and a not-very-bright young woman who aped his nasty remarks. We had also registered the loss of one of our coworkers and friends, Peter Stiasny, who was sent East with one of the transports. After a while, he smuggled out a postcard from a camp near Lodz in which he stated that after arriving in this area, he had been separated from his parents and had never seen them again.

In the neighborhood of the factory were some vegetable growers and gardeners who would sell us their produce at very reasonable prices. We decided to buy for our own use only and not engage in black market trade. When we found out, that one of ours did not abide by this ruling, we were forced to teach him a lesson in giving him the "blanket." After this, he promised never to do it again.

December 7, 1941 brought new developments. The dastardly attack on the American islands of Hawaii by the Japanese resulted in a declaration of war on the Japanese Empire by President Roosevelt in concert with Congress. Germany then declared war on the United States. Now the whole world was embroiled in total war.

For us, a hopeless situation had even turned more hopeless, with no end in sight and the murderous Nazis being victorious on all fronts, chalking up victories day by day.

The "Final Solution" was given to an official Nazi program at a meeting in the Berlin suburb of Wannsee on January 20, 1942. The chairman of the meeting was Reinhard

Heydrich, deputy to Heinrich Himmler, chief of the SS. He reminded the 15 Nazi bureaucrats who attended that he had been authorized to organize a "complete solution to the Jewish question." The purpose of this meeting, he said, was to coordinate the efforts of all relevant ministries, departments and agencies in implementing this task.

Heydrich presented a country-by-country breakdown of the 11 million Jews he estimated were still living in Europe, including Spain, England, Portugal, Switzerland and Sweden. According to the notes kept by Eichmann, his expert in Jewish affairs, Heydrich announced that all Jews would be taken to camps in the East "for labor utilization." He declared, that "doubtless a large part will fall away through natural reduction," adding that the survivors "will have to be dealt with appropriately."

The killing, off course, had already begun. By the time of the conference, more than a million Jews, Slavs and others had been shot, gassed or killed through overwork, starvation or disease. But most of these murderous efforts had been locally organized, particularly on the Eastern front. The Wannsee meeting signaled the beginning of a systematic and unprecedented program designed to exterminate an entire people.

The killings that had already begun had spread like an octopus throughout occupied Europe. Following the defeat of Poland in September 1939, the Nazis began concentrating the Jews into ghettos that isolated them from the outside world. Many were surrounded by barbed wire or brick walls. A ghetto typically was created in the dirtiest, poorest and most crowded section of a city, where passage in and out was strictly controlled. In Warsaw, more than 400,000 Jews were crammed into the largest of ghettos. The Nazi slogan would be: "A race of lower standing needs less room."

With the start of war with the Soviet Union, more territory where Jews had lived for centuries fell into Nazi hands. The killing commandos, following immediately behind the army, were supported by local volunteers and augmented by Ukrainians, Lithuanians, Estonians and Letts serving in SS battalions. They exceeded excellence in the task of shooting Jews and burying them in prepared ditches.

Most of my relatives disappeared in the first few weeks of the German onslaught. My grandfather, Bernard Glanzmann, was shot in his own yard after he asked the Nazi officer to do him the "favor," as the Nazis had already taken his sons. This scene was witnessed by my Uncle Daniel and his wife Regina, standing behind an open door, holding their baby daughter, Dora, in their arms. Following this experience, they left the infant on the doorsteps of a cloister and were hidden by a local farmer, who risked being put to death if they were discovered. They survived and were able to recover Dora after the war.

The other "hold-outs" were Uncle Leo, his wife Regina and daughter Sophie, who hid in cemeteries, churches and other public places and were able to survive the war.

Other relatives, like my father's brother Carl and his wife Ruszia were sent from Vienna to the Lodz ghetto. His sister Adele and her husband Morris Katz disappeared somewhere in Lublin.

To this end, a whole organization had been established to arrest, process and ship off approximately 1,000 people each week to Destination East.

The transports that had started with a trickle were now going full force. It had become only a question of time when it would be our turn to join the ranks of the many thousands who had gone before. Relatives and friends disappeared at an alarming rate, never to be heard from again.

The apartment we lived in was in the sixth district of the city, not in a predominantly Jewish neighborhood where arrests of Jewish people had become a daily happening.

This apartment was in a luxury building owned by the family of Mautner-Markhof, the condiment people. The size of this palatial place was immense, with seven large rooms, a number of smaller rooms and a large entrance hall that doubled as parlor, where Mrs. Mautner held court and Mr. Mautner scurried around, fulfilling all her wishes and giving in to all her whims.

All the rooms, according to the law of that time, had to be sublet. Before long we had a population explosion in this apartment, with all the rooms occupied by a different Jewish family.

Linke Wienzeile 2-4

One of the smaller rooms had been leased to a couple with marital difficulties. On a Sunday morning, while the wife had gone out, the husband committed suicide by hanging, while their large white dog "Balta" sat by watching her master kill himself.

Since Jews were not allowed to have a telephone and the suicide had to be reported to the police, another man and I went across the hall to ask permission to use the phone. There were only two apartments on each floor and this apartment across the hall was a bordello. Girls were peeking out of every cubicle and a very nice lady wearing a multi-colored jacket (whom I took to be the madam) gave us permission to use the phone.

When the police arrived, they were astounded to find a Jewish apartment right in the center of town, although a recent decree required all Jewish apartments to be identified with a black Star of David on white background affixed to the front door.

In their opinion, this area should have been cleared of Jews a long time before, although, according to the laws that are still in effect today all residents had to be registered with the police within 24 hours of establishing residency. By filling out this document, one was also required to answer the question of one's religious affiliation.

Around the middle of April 1942, Germany was jubilantly preparing for the Führer's 50th birthday, with banners, buntings and flags decorating the cities, highways and byways.

Our group met nearly every Sunday afternoon for a discussion in the apartment of Engineer Bauer, a Revisionist Zionist who wrote a number of books. That particular Sunday, when I left Engineer Bauer's place on the Tuchlauben, I had this distinct premonition that this would be my last visit — and that on April 20, the big Hitler birthday, I would definitely not be around.

6. Journey to Hell

The Gestapo would surround a building, block all entrances and exits and proceed to clear the house of all Jewish inhabitants, giving them an hour or two to pack. The Nazis would then load them on open lorries and bring them to temporary quarters in a school building for processing. When they had approximately 1,000 people, they would load them on trains and send them off.

My thoughts were occupied in anticipation of terrible things to happen. What was to be? What does the future have in store for me and my family? Yes I was scared, for the future of all of us. The rumors that we are marked for death cannot be true! People could in reality not be so cruel. It is not possible that a nation that produced a Schiller and a Goethe could have fallen so low. On the other hand, if there is an ounce of truth in this hearsay, will I be able to escape the coming events — or will the coming events crush all of us?

The noose became tighter day by day and the dragnet spread all over the city.

The action by the Gestapo was referred to as *ausheben*, freely translated as being "lifted out." So it did not come as a big surprise when around the 15th or the 16th of April, the agents surrounded our apartment house and arrested all Jewish occupants. All but the Mautners, who had disappeared.

It is very difficult to describe the feeling and thoughts

that went through my mind. The horror of waiting was over, but the horror of the unknown was just beginning. I must admit that I took this moment quite calmly. The thought that struck me was that we are like sheep being led to slaughter. In retrospect, I was not too far off the reality.

We packed our belongings in suitcases marked with big, white letters depicting the name and the city of origin. It was dark by the time we finished. Loaded on open trucks, under armed guard, we made our way past the opera house, through the center of town that looked eerie in the blackout, passing all the familiar streets and places, all the little nooks and crannies that I had known for the first 16 years of my life. I wondered: would I see all this, ever again?

Große Sperlgasse 2

In no time we arrived at the temporary detention center, which was in a high school in the second district, Sperlgasse, in a building with controlled access. It was recessed between two apartment buildings with an iron gate closing off the school courtyard from the alley way that led to the street. An armed SS man guarded the entrance.

The truck pulled into the courtyard and the iron gates closed with a bang. Our luggage was taken away and we could keep just one satchel. We were told not to worry — our luggage would be returned once we reach our final destination.

We were assigned to a classroom in this building, where all the floors of the rooms had been laid out with mattresses. This would be our home for the next few days.

Roaming through the building, I saw a woman in a

multi-colored jacket. When I approached her, I was face-to-face with the lady I thought to be the madam from across the hall. She explained that she had hidden in the bordello but ran into the Gestapo when she went to visit relatives in the second district and was arrested with all other Jews in that particular apartment house.

My sister Mary and I were visited by a Mr. Donat, who was sent by the Jewish Community Council. He instructed us to form Zionist cells wherever we went and to maintain a Zionist Youth movement to keep the youth vibrant and alive. (Little did he know, what was to come!)

In exploring all floors and rooms, I was not surprised to find a soldier in German uniform, with all the insignias removed, crying as a detainee. He probably could not come up with three non-Jewish grandmothers.

Julius Streicher

We were also visited by correspondents and photographers from the Stürmer, the violently anti-Semitic newspaper edited by Julius Streicher, who for crimes against humanity was found guilty and executed at Nuremberg. These correspondents were looking for "typical" Jews to film and photograph. They took pictures of two men and made them whisper into each others ear, until they thought they had taken the "perfect" picture. After they had left, we asked one of the fellows what he had whispered in his companion's ear. He said that he told him, "They can kiss my ass."

Soon all the rooms were filled to overflowing and everybody had to report to a commission.

We were lined up to report to this commission of high-ranking SS officers when they apparently had enough people for that particular transport and we were told that our turn would come the next time. It arrived on May 6, 1942. It was a simple procedure: They took away our identity cards with the red "J" and stamped the card "evacuated."

Now we had nothing — no possessions, no identity, no name. Nothing.

In the third district, there were a number of slaughter-houses. Like the Chicago stockyards, they were serviced by a net of rails and railroad depots.

Under the cover of darkness, we were loaded on trucks and brought to the rail yard. We were loaded into regular but old Pullman cars, eight people to each compartment, to start our journey to the East. The Jewish Community Council had provided us with box-type food packages, a pleasant surprise. We were told that we were to be sent to the Minsk ghetto.

Our journey started that very night and took us through the former Czechoslovakia, through Moravia and Bohemia, through the mountains of the Sudetenland, which was excitingly beautiful by moonlight. Forests and waterfalls made the panorama complete.

Soon we entered the former Polish territories and passed

through Czenstochova, Krakow and Warsaw. On the road between Warsaw and Brest-Litovsk, we saw Jewish prisoners working near the rails. As we threw some edibles out the window, they cried out and warned us, that we were doomed to die. We could not understand why they would say such a thing. Who could believe or wanted to believe these people?

388	Seiler Alfred Israel	G.L.Tienveile 4/9	14.2. 26
380	Seiler Chaje Ester Sara	"	2.10.96
401	Seiler Mary Sara	"	34.8. 23
379	Seiler Wolf Israel	"	19.12.96

Soon our trip would be over. If all continued to go as it had, it wouldn't be so bad. When we crossed the former German-Soviet border at Brest-Litovsk, the train stopped at a siding. Night had fallen and we lulled ourselves to sleep. Suddenly, like an explosion, the doors of the compartments of the train were ripped open and SS men, accompanied by large, barking dogs, started screaming on top of their voices: "Raus, Raus, Raus!" We had to leave the train and run across the unlit dark platform to waiting cattle cars. People were screaming, children crying, families were separated, luggage was lost and SS men were beating the not-so-swift with their riding crops, adding to the confusion that ensued. Within minutes the boxcars were loaded with approximately 60 people to each car and after receiving two pails of water, the doors were shut and sealed.

Our journey continued now under quite different circumstances. The train would travel all night and stand on a rail siding all day. A couple of days later, pushed again onto an unused side rail, we were permitted to leave our "prison coach" to stretch our legs in a limited area and surrounded by SS men. As soon as I got off, I and another three or four young men were given shovels and instructed to dig a grave for four people who had died on the transport. The ground was very hard and the time given us was very short, so we dug a very shallow grave and buried these unlucky people. This was my first encounter with death.

The train chugged along the last few miles toward Minsk. What did we really know about Minsk? That it was the capital of the Soviet Republic of White Russia, Byelorussia. Minsk was overrun and occupied in the first week of the war. After twenty years of Soviet rule, there were no longer any Jewish neighborhoods in Minsk. Jews resided in all parts of the city, in the urban and suburban districts.

Minsk Ghetto

As soon as the Germans occupied Minsk, an order was issued to establish a ghetto.

Long lines headed toward the area that had been designated as the ghetto. Not to report was punishable by death. Masses of Jews who fled on foot were overtaken by the advancing enemy army and fell into the hands of the murderers. Posters announced that "a hundred Jew-Bolsheviks had been shot." Or as the case might be, 20 or 30, but every day brought new executions and new orders. A new order decreed that all men between 15 and 45 must register immediately. As usual, failure to register was punishable by death.

On every street, soldiers with metal "half moons" around their necks searched and seized men and boys indiscriminately. From outward appearances, Germans could not tell who was a Jew and who was not, so all those rounded up were sent to a camp outside the city at Drozdy.

Approximately 14,000 men were ordered to sit in an open field at Drozdy under the blazing sun. Anyone trying to stand was shot. Men died of thirst, but the slightest movement toward a nearby stream drew immediate machine-gun fire.

Several days later came the order to separate the Jews. At first the Jewish prisoners did not realize the intent of the order. Only a few sensed the danger and did not obey the decree. They stayed and were "covered" by Byelorussian or Russian friends. On the fifth day, all civilians except Jews were allowed to go free. Then came the order to separate Jews with "educated" professions from the mass of other prisoners. People thought, the Germans would put the Jewish engineers, technicians, architects, physicians and artists to work. About 3,000 Jews reported in this category.

Black Raven

The next order was very surprising. All physicians and hospital workers were ordered to separate themselves from the rest of the "intellectuals." No one anticipated what awaited the rest. It never occurred to anyone that the first objective of the Nazis was to get rid of people who might lead resistance movements. The Jews did not understand why this small group of doctors was sent back into the mass of the other prisoners. From their experience in Warsaw and other ghettos in Poland, the Germans knew that epidemics might break out as a result of crowded conditions and the starvation in the Jewish quarters. They were deathly afraid of the spread of epidemics outside the ghetto. For the time being, the doctors were spared.

Not until they were on the road out of Drozdy did the Jewish intellectuals realize that they were not being taken to Minsk but in the opposite direction. They were headed for a death camp in Trostenez, where immediate death awaited. Many were suffocated along the way in the Dush-egupky, the gassing van. The Dushegupkies, which we later called the "Black Raven," were specially equipped vans driven by diesel engines. The exhaust was piped back into the inside of the closed and sealed body of the truck. The word Dushegupky translated means "soul-extinguisher."

At Trostenez, the bodies were piled up and burned. The Jewish intellectuals were thus among the first victims of the Nazi mass-murder machine. The rumor that the Nazis spread was that these men had been taken from Drozdy to various labor camps and that they would send word soon of their whereabouts.

This was the picture and situation in Minsk at the time of our arrival.

The train came to an abrupt halt in an open field, and within seconds the doors of the boxcars were ripped open in the manner now familiar to us. SS men equipped with riding crops, were screaming "Raus, Raus," their dogs barking and tearing on the leashes, showing their fangs, ready to jump at the next human being, hoping to be let loose but restrained by their masters. The whole area was surrounded by gun-toting SS guards of Baltic origin.

We were not allowed to take any of our belongings with us and the thousand or so people had to line up in front of the train. As we were standing and waiting, an SS officer came to select a number of young men, including me, to stay behind and unload the train.

The rest of the people were loaded onto trucks of all kinds, including Dushegupkies, and driven away.

Soon the trucks came back and we started to unload the boxcars, which took our group most of the afternoon and well into the night. One of the SS guards came to one of our boys and confiscated his wristwatch. When the young man complained, he was told not to worry because "where you are going, there are big clocks on the walls."

It must have been around 10 or 11 at night, when we finished unloading. Now, we were put on a lorry and transported to SS headquarters in Minsk. There, lined up in two rows, we were told to wait. It gave me time to think: What will be happening to us? Where are my parents and where is my sister? Will I ever see them again? How did we as individuals and as a people get into this hopeless situation? Are there any answers? My thoughts seesawed between hope and despair. What was our crime to be treated worse than criminals? What was to come?

I had lost all concept of time when an SS officer came out from one of the buildings and handed each one of us a loaf of bread. I felt elated. If they had planned to kill us, (did I think "kill"?), they would not have wasted a loaf of bread. A loaf of bread meant that we would live another day.

7. Maly Trostenez (Malyy Trostenets)

Again loaded on an open truck, we were driven out of the city toward Mogilev. At about 10-12 kilometers outside Minsk, we left the highway and took a dirt road that eventually led to a place with large barns and a silo. Obviously, these were large farm buildings, perhaps it was a former *sovkhoz*, a large farm owned by the state where farmers share all equipment and all land and work for wages. The landscape sloped gently toward a lake. The moon played hide and seek between the clouds and gave the whole panorama an eerie look.

Shoot-to-kill sign

The truck stopped in front of one of the barns. It was kind of a double barn, with an opening in the center and the log-cabin-type construction running perhaps 150 feet to each side. We were told to go into the left side of this building and lie down on the straw-covered ground to catch some sleep. Upon entering in total darkness, the first lad fell over a body. Feeling his way and touching this person, he yelled out: "There are people here"!

68

We found people sleeping around the perimeter of the barn. I had found a flashlight and started to shine the beam on the faces, walking clockwise. I had nearly completed the circle when I found my parents and my sister. When they were led away, the SS had asked for volunteers to repair the dirt road leading from the highway to this place and also to unload the luggage from the trucks. Volunteering for this saved their lives.

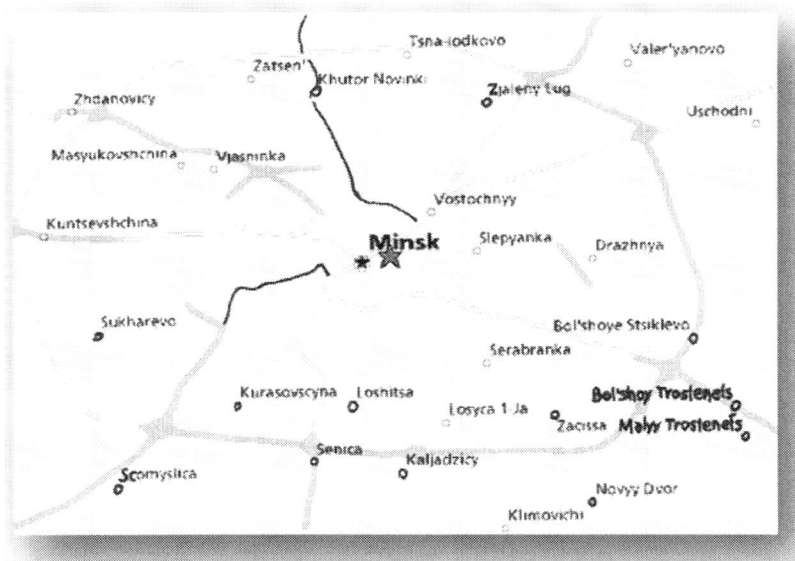

On the next morning, which had come too fast, we were detailed to work. Our transport was the first to come into this camp and the total count, including our railroad work party, comprised of 86 people. When we inquired about the others we were told that they were on other farms, or in other camps, and we would hear from them, soon.

The name of the town, as we found out later, was Maly Trostenez (Maly, meaning small or little). In November 1941, the Minsk Security Police and the SD (Sicherheitsdienst) established a new camp there at a 200 hectares (500-acre) former collective farm named for Karl Marx. Initially the camp was intended to supply the local Nazi forces with food. In addition a mill, sawmill, locksmith's shop, tailor, shoemaker and other workshops were built. Jews and Soviet POWs built barracks for around 600 mainly Jewish slave laborers. The prisoners selected for work in the camp were kept at first in a large barn and in 20 cellars, which were formerly used by the local farmers for cooling potatoes, vegetables and meat. Later they were housed in barracks, where bunks were constructed from thick unshaved wooden planks in three tiers. The camp was surrounded by a threefold barbed wire fence and wooden lookout towers were erected at the corners of the perimeter. A guardroom was located close to the entrance to the camp and machine-gun nests were around the entire site.

The buildings, made out of wooden logs, were in a terrible state of disrepair. The lake ended in a small wooden dam, with a grain mill driven by water power. On the far side of the camp was a wooded area about half a mile wide that lay alongside the fields for about a mile and a half. Neglected fields stretched for at least two miles west of the village and were only interrupted by rails running in a North-South direction. About two to three miles east of the camp was the Minsk-Mogilev Road, a two-lane highway that was connected to the camp by the now famous dirt road that was instrumental in saving the lives of my family.

Most of the buildings, including the silo, had gaping holes and parts of the roofs missing. Some buildings had no walls.

The building where we had spent the first night was now used to unpack the suitcases and sort the personal belongings of all the prisoners. The result was a tremendous warehouse of shoes, clothing, dishes, eyeglasses and food. Valuables had to be separated and were earmarked for Berlin.

As inmates, we were permitted to use any kind of clothing we wanted. But we would be executed if caught trading or selling anything from the magazine, as this barrack was now called.

White Russia had been re-named and was now White

Ruthenia. The entire command structure was headed by SS and Police General Zenner. After February 1942, Zenner was replaced by Obersturmbannführer Edouard Strauch, head of security services in White Ruthenia, who had been sent from Berlin.

The head of the civil administration, which carried out the Hitler policy towards the Jews, was Wilhelm Kube. He was one of the first organizers of Hitler's Nazi Party, son of a Prussian junior officer. He was already a deputy in the Reichstag as early as 1924, representing the ultra-right. In 1928 Kube headed the Nazi faction in the Prussian legislature. At every opportunity he had demonstrated his anti-Semitic position. In a 1935 article on the Jewish question, he wrote in a Western German newspaper: "What plague or tuberculosis or syphilis means for the health of humanity, Jewry means for the way of life of the white races. The carrier of this disease must be isolated and eliminated."

On his staff were a number of high-ranking SS officers, including Sturmbann-führer Madeker, who was in command of our camp with his office in Minsk, and Sturmbannführer Heuser, who was the attorney general of Byelorussia.

The immediate command of the camp rested in the hands of two non-commissioned officers, Herbert Kujan and Heinrich Eiche, with Kujan being in overall charge and Eiche in charge of agriculture.

Every morning we had to line up at the Appell, the daily count, where we received our job assignments. We also had to listen to the remarks and barrages of the commanding officer, Herbert Kujan, and the derogatory remarks he made about his second in command, whom he called "Garden Heini."

Since the barn where we spent our first night was now a workplace, we had been transferred to a former stable. The dirt on the floor was at least two feet high, and we were able to make sleeping quarters by spreading some straw on top of the cow dung and putting mattresses over it. Every transport that came to this camp carried a wagon load of mattresses, so we had plenty of them.

In one corner of this barn was a separate small room, which was occupied by three women: Norma a nurse, who wore a white nurse's uniform and had assumed some kind of command; Hermie a blonde, voluptuous dame; and Julie Hochbaum. Hermie and Julie were in charge of the kitchen.

Apparently the commandant was attracted to the bombshell. Before long, he disappeared and Eiche was put in charge of the camp. Word had it, Commandant Kujan was executed for Rassenschande — racial shame. Much later, Norma and Hermie were taken in handcuffs to Minsk. After a few days, there were brought back into the camp, bloody, beaten, and hardly recognizable. They were executed in front of the whole assembly by hanging on hooks that had been clamped to the light poles.

One of my first assignments was to clear the fields of rocks. We had to collect these big stones and had to hand-carry them to designated areas. I could not understand how the Soviets could grow anything on those neglected acres.

At one time, two of my co-workers and I were chosen to hurriedly dig a grave for an SS officer who had been killed by partisans. Gladly, we rushed down to the forest strip at the end of the camp. We were just about finished as the funeral procession was moving down the hill toward the grave site. We had to hide in the underbrush to avoid being seen. From that time on, we were called often to prepare graves for Germans killed by partisans. Before long, we had created a big cemetery.

My job assignments varied. Sometimes they were simple tasks but always hard and always under the threat of the gun. One of the hardest jobs was the under-plowing of potatoes. We had to walk behind a pair of oxen, guiding the plow between the rows of the spuds. But my motto had become: It cannot last forever; even this will eventually come to an end. I was also assigned to tasks like gleaning, threshing, haying, leveling land, digging foundations for buildings and helping erecting houses for the "gentry." That's where I made the acquaintance of Jews from the ghetto of Minsk and learned to speak Yiddish.

Every day, the Germans would bring a truckload of these Russian Jews from the ghetto into the camp. These Russians were what the Germans would call specialists in woodwork and were detailed to build new buildings and villas for the SS officers. The Germans prepared to stay forever. After all, this was just the beginning of the thousand-year Reich. Their armies stood before Moscow, Leningrad and Stalingrad. They believed it was just a matter of time before they would link up with the Japanese in the middle of Siberia.

Other than with the few Russian Jews that came to work on the buildings, we had no contact with the Jews from the Minsk ghetto.

At one time, Dr. Heuser, the dreaded prosecutor of White Russia, brought two Jewish-German women, a mother and a daughter, into our camp. Who they were and what the connection was between these two Jewish women and this high-ranking SS officer will always remain an enigma to me.

On July 28, 1942, shortly after those two women were brought into the camp, the Russian Jews were kept in the camp for four days while a massacre took place in the ghetto. On July 26, two days before the massacre was to begin, Heinrich Himmler wrote to Berger, head of the office of Race and Emigration: "The occupied Eastern regions will become 'Judenrein' (free of Jews). The Führer has placed the implementation of this very difficult order on my shoulders."

We had tried to settle into a certain routine, but this routine was interrupted by transports arriving every week from Vienna or Prague. Every transport yielded a few people with selected special trades that were added to the camp population and others. People from our camp who had been either sick or injured were sent to "other" camps in exchange. When their clothing arrived back in the camp within a short time, the unthinkable truth was confirmed. All the rumors were not rumors at all. It stared us square into the face. There were no other camps and there were

definitely no other farms. There were only killing fields. When would our turn come? We were sentenced to death for a crime not committed. We were on death row, and our appeal was in the hands of every German — or for that matter, every Ukrainian, Lett, Estonian or Lithuanian in a German uniform with a gun.

They had stripped us of everything. We had only a shirt on our back and even this did

Mass murder

not belong to us.

The population in our camp—truly a slave labor camp— had grown to about 600 people whose job was to supply the gentry with all necessities and comforts possible. After lining up every morning for the daily count, we were grouped into labor parties and marched off to our work places.

At that time, I worked at cutting boards out of trees by hand. A tree would be marked with charcoal and then lifted on a tall saw horse, with one man standing on the top of the now horizontal tree and two men below. The saw had handles on each end. We could thus cut about a tree a day and produce five to six boards daily.

It was still summer or perhaps early fall when we saw the luggage of my Aunt Anna, my father's oldest sister, in the midst of suitcases trucked into the camp. She was one of the martyrs killed along with all the other people on this particular transport.

Horst Böhm was the leader of a work party cutting bog. The call for "general Appell" indicated that something bad was going to happen. We were all lined up when Horst and his group were brought into the camp. The boys were caught swapping clothing for food. Three of them were commanded to kneel down and executed on the order of Eiche by an SS man, who shot them in the back of their necks. When it came to Horst Böhm, Eiche said to him: "Oh I see, you ran a whole trade organization!" Böhm calmly replied: "No, we did not run a trade organization, we just exchanged some old clothing for bread because we were hungry!"

Eiche replied: "You die like a man, standing up straight." With that, the SS man shot Horst with a bullet in the back of the neck.

Heinrich Eiche

Eiche was a Volks Deutscher from Riga, Latvia who had a lamp and electric parts store in Riga before the war. Soon after the execution of Böhm, Eiche was replaced by a Schupo (policeman) named Richard Tosch, born in Berlin on November 12, 1909. This sick bastard would kill people at random. He would just pull out his gun from the holster, aim and fire.

By then we had established a number of workshops, like a tailor shop, which was under the direction of Mr. Preminger, who looked and spoke like his famous brother Otto. This tailor shop made uniforms to measure for the high-ranking SS officers and also repaired bloody and torn uniforms returned from the front.

The tanner and shoemaker Mr. Schneider was making high-grade boots for the SS staff. The laundry was in service to wash clothing for the troops.

Toward the end of August, it became known that the

Germans had been encircled at Stalingrad, the city on the Volga (today's Volgograd). At the same time, our blacksmith received orders to make 36-inch hooks with a round handle on one end. Subsequently, the Germans or the Latvians in German service stationed in the camp would ride out every morning. By midday or early afternoon, fires would be burning all around the area. They dug up the murdered people from their mass graves and burned them, so as not leave any evidence.

When electric power was brought into the camp, the Germans set out to modernize the work place.

With one of the transports came a big, husky man named Diamant who spoke Russian fluently. He fit into the plans of the commandant and he was given special permission and a truck with an SS man as a driver to drive into Minsk and to trade clothing for machinery. He bought all kinds of woodworking machinery, circular saws, a shingle-making machine, electric motors in all sizes. Most important to us: He connected with the German bakery in town and would buy broken pieces of bread, helping to alleviate hunger in the camp.

The liquidation of the ghetto of Slutzk provided the SS with a saw mill that they brought into the camp. To dismantle the mill, they had taken along four of our people: Rosenberg, the blacksmith; Diamant, and two others. The sawmill was covered with the blood of the innocent martyrs who were killed by the SS in the liquidation of the ghetto.

Stables with horses provided the gentry with the pleasures of a country club, as well as the orgies that were held in the company of Russian women turncoats.

Meanwhile Tosch had shot to death a young man named Paul, who was in charge of the cow shed, because he was urinating on the pile of dung behind the stables. He also executed two men at the morning lineup — Mr. Banaschek and another whose name I have forgotten — because they sold their own watches to Russian peasants. Emil Kleiner was shot and killed for trying to smuggle a letter of his whereabouts to Vienna. A woman was killed with the command "umlegen" (lie down) on the spot when she failed to take her hands out of her apron pockets during an inspection by the head of the civil administration of occupied Byelorussia, Wilhelm Kube. (He was later killed by partisans who planted a bomb under his bed.)

My friend Yoshko Pollack came to the camp with his father, Eugene, from Prague. Yoshko, who spoke some Russian, was put to work in the flour mill. Every day the local Russians would come to "his" mill with grain, and for a charge of 5% he was authorized to mill their wheat. Sometime around the middle or end of 1942, Yoshko told me he could purchase two guns.

I got some money together and with both our resources we bought two guns. Mine was a "Politrook 1936" that I carried on the inside of my boots with my working pants over it. I felt a little more secure carrying this weapon. I thought: If they get me, I can take a few with me.

About that time, Tosch left and was replaced by Scharführer (Group Leader) Rieder, an Austrian from the town of Kufstein who swore no one would touch a hair on any of "my Jews' heads" because his wife used to work for a Jewish doctor who had treated her so well.

The killings within the camp had stopped after more than half of our population was "evacuated" and shipped West. (I presume that they were shipped to Auschwitz).

I had contracted jaundice, and my people hid me on a cot set up under the roof in the magazine, where I could peek out in the open and watch the comings and goings. It was winter, the underbrush had lost its leaves and I had a clear vision of the strip of forest from my hiding place. I could see a "Black Raven" unload his cargo of dead, leaving them on the ground in the woods.

About that time our people were ordered to build a bunker, I never saw it, but I was told that it was a rectangular hole, about 30 to 40 feet long, about 20 to 30 feet wide and about four to five feet deep. The walls and the floor were covered in cement. The bunker was constructed in the small strip of forest bordering the camp, near the German cemetery. To this bunker, they would truck uncounted numbers of people. When the trucks passed the sawmill, they would be boarded by Rieder with a machine pistol slung over his shoulder. Shortly after they arrived at the bunker, we could hear the gun volleys. After pouring gasoline over the dead, he would toss an incendiary grenade into the bunker. The smell of burning flesh would permeate the camp.

This went on day after day, with no end in sight. While we were working in the saw mill, a German army unit came to us to cut lumber for them, which we were permitted to

Killing pit, shown after liberation

do for a 5 per cent commission. As I stood outside the building preparing the next tree to be cut, a German officer asked what those funny-looking trucks were. When we told him that they were used to kill people, he wouldn't or couldn't believe it. (What normal human being could!)

Once I was called upon to clean and wash the inside of a death wagon. The sight of these trucks was nauseating. Clumps of hair and blood covered the inside walls and the stench of urine was overwhelming.

My chronology might be a little awry, but it was common knowledge that the German forces had suffered a number of defeats on the Eastern front, that they had capitulated in Stalingrad and that they were retreating in the face of the Soviet advances.

Within the camp, nothing had changed for the moment; only more trucks were passing by, filled to capacity with people to be executed by Rieder. Occasionally Eiche was also seen to accompany the death vehicles.

Worthwhile to mention is the heroic stand taken by our "doctor," Paul Meyer, actually a medical student from Prague. We were given permission to reconstruct the silo into a camp hospital. When typhoid fever broke out, we were afraid the whole camp would be executed. Paul, standing in front of the hospital, was asked during an inspection if there were any sick people inside. He answered that he was happy to report there were none. In fact, he had eight or nine people with typhoid fever on the upper floor.

A number of incidents had taken place. When the Germans played with a hand grenade and it would not explode, they had instructed one of our people to take the "hot" grenade and toss it into the lake, which he did to the amusement of the SS men. Or the random shooting of work parties returning from a day's labor on the fields. Once my work party was shot at with machine gun fire. I felt the bullets whistling by my ear and I could feel the heat of the bullet. At another time a girl returning from the fields was shot to death. I was beaten and kicked a number of times, but one beating stands out in my memory. I was hit in the face by an SS man with brass knuckles, missing my left eye by millimeters, for not greeting him in the proper manner by taking off my cap and standing at attention.

But the worst thing of all was not knowing what they had up their sleeves. For that matter one could have gotten killed any day or night by an attack of the Soviet Air Force, which had started bombing raids on Minsk and the surrounding areas.

The Germans had brought a locomobile into the camp, which was promptly destroyed during a Soviet air attack.

Next to the sawmill, the Russian Jews erected a building to house all the wood-working machines that Mr. Diamant had acquired during his buying trips to Minsk. In this building, a straight stairway led up to the second floor to the residence of the commandant Rieder. It became known that he stored incendiary grenades that he used for his special task in his entrance or ante-room.

I had decided that the time had come to do away with him. I thought it to be an opportunity of a lifetime. I would just walk up the stairs, surprise him and shoot him to death, then set the building afire by using one of his grenades.

My plan was negated by the elders, who argued that the whole camp would suffer the consequences — and perhaps the whole camp population would be executed.

We were informed of the goings-on in the outside world partially from smuggled-in newspapers and also from snatching bits of news walking by the SS barracks when their radios were turned on. We became aware of the uprising in the Warsaw Ghetto when one of our women found a letter in a shirt pocket that was to be washed in the camp laundry. It stated "that we are fighting the Jews in the Warsaw ghetto now for seven days."

In the early months of 1944, the distinct sound of cannon fire could be heard from far away and it was about that time that the Soviets had started their offensive against the German intruders. The Germans had been beaten back and were retreating on all fronts.

An overseer was suddenly posted at the saw mill, watching us at all times. He was a little man, a Ukrainian civilian who could hardly speak ten words of German. He would greet any German that came near the mill with an outstretched arm and yell on top of his lungs, "Khail Khitler." It was obvious that the Germans were amused by his outbreaks and tirades. We did our utmost to ignore him and whenever possible put him in his place.

The spring brought news from the front. The Germans had been beaten near Smolensk and the Russians were advancing on a broad front.

As if not to lose any time, all gold, silver and other valuables of all the murdered Jewish people who had come to Minsk were crated and shipped to Berlin in care of the Reichskommissar for Jewish properties.

On June 6, commandant Rieder addressed us at the morning line-up and announced that the Americans and British had landed on the shores of France. He insisted this was the plan of the Führer, who had decided to let them in and then destroy them once and for all. Rieder again assured us that "my Jews" have nothing to fear.

On the 28th day of June, the SK 27 (Special Commandos) arrived in the camp. They looked like murderers, which they were. It was obvious why they had come.

After working as usual at the saw mill all day, I and a few others were ordered to work through the night loading ammunition that was stored in a building within the camp. We were loading grenades and other projectiles unto trucks and as soon as one truck pulled out, another truck would take its place to be loaded to capacity.

One could see that the Germans were jittery, but the murder vans and open trucks, loaded with hundreds of human beings, kept moving by unabated. The people brought now to the execution site were no longer Jews; they were Russians or White Russians. Rieder made no secret of what he had been doing all along. At one time he proudly told us at one of the morning roll-calls that one woman had shaken his hand and had said: "Do svidaniya" (So long, or till I see you again), which he found to be so very amusing.

8. Escape

The dawn broke on a hot, cloudless summer day — the 29th of June 1944. We were lined up at the morning's roll-call and proceeded to our designated work places. Although I hadn't slept for 24 hours, I took time to change my clothing to be ready for any and all eventualities. I wore an extra shirt and another pair of slacks, with my gun safely tucked inside my boots.

I had decided along with my parents and sister that the time had come to take our destiny into our own hands. There was obviously nothing to lose, since everything pointed to our execution.

At about 8:30 that morning, we were exposed to another speech by the commandant. He stood on a pile of trees in front of the sawmill, emphasizing again he would not harm any of us.

My father's brother Carl had a son-in-law named Hans Amschel, who was standing nearby as we were ready to escape. When I told him to come with us, he turned to me with tears in his eyes and said, "My Scharführer promised me that he would not harm us and I believe him." (He, his wife who was my cousin Jenny and their daughter Eva, did not survive.)

We saw that there were no SS guards manning the watch towers, and we knew it was time to leave. We were joined by Julie Hochbaum as well as Yoshko and his father. We agreed to meet at a certain point outside the compound on the road leading toward the railroad tracks, where there was a dip in the road and a deep ditch provided cover.

As I approached the hideout, I was perturbed not to see my mother, who was to have left the camp ahead of me. After waiting a few minutes, I went back into the lion's den and found her in the magazine. She told me the commandant had ordered her to furnish dresses, shoes and other clothing for a few Russian women who had been working for the Germans. I said, "Leave everything and come. Tell these women to help themselves and take what they want."

Rejoining the group, we walked toward the rail line and were about to cross it when a column of men with horses and wagons cut across out path. They were Black Police — Russians in German service who wore black uniforms with gray epaulets. At the same time, a German squad car carrying SS officers came toward us. The Russians motioned us to come quickly to them and they surrounded us, as not to be seen by the SS men in the Jeep-like car. They also told us to remove the yellow stars we were still wearing. After the Germans passed, they wished us luck and sent us on our way.

The wheat stood high, which enabled us to make our way through the fields without being seen. We walked for hours, coming close to villages where we could see and hear the Germans working and loading trucks. We were worn out when we found an old trench on top of a rise. We slipped into it, hoping to rest, but hail and rain began to come down in buckets and continued incessantly throughout the whole night.

This was not the worst thing to happen. A German tank battalion bivouacked all around us. We heard them talk and discuss their situation. We had to keep completely quiet and still.

Below us was a creek, spanned by a damaged wooden bridge. The German soldiers repaired it throughout the night, enabling the tank column to move out early in the morning.

Overlooking the landscape, we saw the area ringed by forests, which could provide us with an excellent cover. In the distance we saw a forest with comparatively young trees. Knowing that the Germans had strict orders not to venture into the woods because the Russians partisans were in control, we proceeded to this area as fast as we could.

Along the way we passed another village where the Germans were busy loading trucks, obviously preparing for their retreat.

At last we reached our temporary destination and found a hideout in a depression, girded by almost impregnable bushes and young trees. Once settled in, we had time to discuss our situation and seek ways of supplying us with food. For the moment, our only nourishment was the leftover hail, not thawed under the low branches of some needle trees.

The next day, Yoshko and I ventured to the very end of the forest, where we were suddenly confronted by two Russian youngsters. They thought we were parachutists or partisans. We explained that we were Jews escaping from the German concentration camp, hiding out and waiting for liberation by the Red Army. We implored them to keep our meeting secret. With that, they left for their village but returned later that afternoon accompanied by their fathers. They brought us bread and boiled potatoes, a large can filled with water, and shaving equipment, including a mirror.

During the night, the Germans blew up an ammunition depot, apparently not far from our hiding place. Thick smoke covered the whole area, making it nearly impossible to breathe.

An army detachment retreated through the woods and made us scatter in all directions. After they left, we went back to our hide-out and found our water can kicked over and all the water spilled.

Early one morning, after a week or so in our encampment, our two Russian youngsters came running to inform us that the unbelievable had happened: The Nazis were gone and the Red Army was approaching.

Was it possible that we had survived this nightmare?

Was it possible that we are free? Is this what freedom tastes like? Does the air really smell sweeter? A million thoughts rushed through my head. Will the Russians recognize our suffering and send us home right after they defeat this scourge of mankind? What is expected of us next?

What was expected from us was to follow the invitation of our Russian friends and accompany them into their hamlet. Like a dream, we walked into the village to be welcomed by the inhabitants lining both sides of the street and applauding our entry.

We felt like human beings again. We were treated to an evening meal and put up in a house. From the posters that lay torn on the floor and the pictures trampled on the ground, it must have been the quarters of the German commandant. Yoshko and I buried our guns in an adjacent barn because we thought the Russians would have too many questions for two "foreign" young men carrying weapons.

A barren valley lay between this village and the main road, where we saw the first advance units of the Red Army the next morning. Elated, we rushed down into the valley to greet our liberators. Two Russian soldiers raced toward us with their machine pistols at the ready. When they came closer, the one farther away opened fire, only to hit his companion. I helped him give first aid to the wounded man and applied bandages to the man's injured back.

An officer saw this commotion and came riding up on his horse, demanding to know who we were and where we were hiding. We asked him to send us to wherever we could obtain identity papers. He suggested we make our way to the village of Novy Dvor, where some kind of civilian control, perhaps even the Soviet General staff, should be quartered by now.

After thanking our hosts, we made our way to Novy Dvor, only to be confronted by a detachment of Nazi soldiers coming towards us on motor bikes. The street was flanked by big, old oak trees. Behind each stood a Soviet soldier, waiting for the Germans to come nearer. Faced by the Russians, the Teutons raised their arms in surrender. Their boots and watches were immediately liberated by their captors.

Fearing a counter attack by the forces of evil, we fled with the local population toward Minsk. The captured Nazis were guarded by two Russian soldiers and chased along the ditch that ran alongside the road. When the Nazis started to slow down, in apparent anticipation of a German counter attack, the Russians opened fire and killed all of them. The local women picked up big rocks and smashed the German's heads so that their brains splattered all over the landscape.

On the way to Minsk, we passed a burning building that had been the headquarters of the Russian Black Police. We were told that this building was set afire with all the police inside and none of them escaped. In front of this edifice I saw a policeman in his black uniform, draped over the stump of a tree with a bayonet stuck in his back.

Vlassov, a Russian general, surrendered to the Germans in the first week of the armed conflict. He was instrumental in founding an army to fight against his own countrymen. He would scout prisoner of war camps, or would find conscripts within the dissatisfied masses of his own people, yearning to be freed from living under the boot of Communism. An outgrowth of this army, which served under the SS insignia, was the Black Police They were notorious for carrying out Aktionen (actions) in the ghetto and were known for their cruelty in dealing with Jews.

In the very beginning of the German occupation, the Ukrainians and Russians had welcomed the Germans with bread and salt as liberators. But when the Nazis began to treat the inhabitants as Untermenschen (sub-humans), the natives formed fighting groups known as the partisans. They attacked installations important to the war effort; they attacked Germans wherever they could find them, and cut the German supply lines. A number of Jews who escaped from the ghetto were instrumental in some of the defeats handed to the occupying army.

Minsk in ruins

Upon entering Minsk, we asked for direction to headquarters and were immediately put under the gun until questioned. Following some directions, we saw an area of utter destruction and were told that this is where the ghetto used to be. Not one house was left standing.

Not finding any authority or any civilian in charge, we bivouacked in an undamaged building in the center of town. We were resting in the lobby when a number of officers with big red stars and gold braids on their caps and red stripes on their pants entered the building. They rushed past us and went upstairs. After a few minutes, they came down and left the lobby. One officer remained and asked what kind of people we were. We explained that we had escaped from a concentration camp. In a very soft voice, he said: "Ind mamme-lushion kennt ihr?" (And do you speak your mother's tongue?) I can still hear my mother crying out: "A Yid!" He turned to his driver and ordered him to bring all the food he had. Ivan, the driver said: "But Comrade General, there is only enough food for you!" He said: "Never mind, give them everything there is."

This was a royal meal of a sort we had not eaten in ages – bread with real butter, baked chicken, eggs, apples and milk.

He suggested that we leave the city and go east, because of German air raids and a possible German counter attack, which seemed imminent. Listening to his advice, we left the city the next morning, crossing over a destroyed bridge. We had to climb down on one side, then jump over the flowing water in the middle and then pull ourselves up on the other side. Many of the local people had left with us, trying to escape a German counter punch that never materialized.

We were just one small group of refugees trekking east, just one little speck within the masses of people, which must have numbered in the thousands. Tired and hungry, we would rest alongside the road, not knowing where we would sleep the following night, nor did we know where our next meal would come from.

At one of our roadside stops, I witnessed the display of the famous "Katusha" rocket, known also as the "Stalin organ." Mounted on a truck, this thing was capable of firing sixteen rockets every eight seconds, repeatedly. The Russians had surrounded a German battalion and had fired the rockets into this wooded area until the Nazis raised the white flag in surrender.

A Russian soldier nearby had opened a can of American-made stew, which he devoured as I watched. When he was finished and discarded the can, I picked it up and had a meal from the leftovers.

I was amazed to see that the trucks rolling toward the front were mostly American-made Studebakers and Fords. The Russian trucks were known as ZIS, for the first letters of Zavod Imeni Stalina (Factory in Stalin's Name). They were decorated with Stalin's picture and all were in a sorry state of disrepair.

In some places, houses were still afire; the electric overhead wires would be down, dancing and sparking on the ground.

At some point, we decided to head for Moscow. We were positive there must be embassies in exile representing our countries and we were sure to get some identity papers from an Austrian envoy in charge.

We were arrested and questioned whenever we entered a village or town. Sometimes we were held overnight, only to be released the following morning. When that occurred, we demanded to be fed, since it was "unheard of not to feed prisoners." At other times, the arrests were quite scary. Once we were held by a soldier with his gun cocked and ready to shoot until he was stopped at the last moment by his superior officer.

One night, we were lucky to find lodging in an abandoned camp and find a roof over our heads in an old dilapidated barrack. As soon as we settled in, we were awakened by men in uniform and forced to load barrels of oil onto a train that was obviously destined for the front.

Between walking and thumbing rides on anything that was moving East, we reached Borisov on the Bersina. When we came to Borisov, some local people told us that out of a large Jewish population — I seem to remember the figure being about 75,000 — only one Jewish woman survived, and that was only because she was married to a non-Jewish Russian.

I don't remember how long we remained in Borisov, but we were about to cross the Beresina toward Moscow when a women came running after us. She was that one Jewish survivor. She had come to meet us and she wanted to give us something, so she brought a meatloaf with eggs baked into it (Russian style). After telling her about our experiences and after spending some time with her and thanking her for her gift, we parted company and went our way.

In front of the bridge spanning the Beresina was a plaza. There we saw our friend the Soviet general who fed us before suggesting we leave Minsk. Upon recognizing us, he again ordered his chauffeur to supply as with all edibles he carried in his car. He also provided us with a paper, which ordered "all moving stock traveling East to help and assist this group of seven people in any way and to provide transport at any time." This paper was signed by our Jewish friend, who turned out to be the "Commanding Officer of all Highways and Railroads on the Third White Russian Front."

With this paper in our hand, we crossed the Beresina, the river where Napoleon I was decidedly defeated in the famous "Battle on the Beresina" while retreating from Moscow in 1812.

I was grateful to the Russians for saving my life. I even flirted with the idea of embracing Communism as an answer to all the world's ills. But the farther I came into the hinterland, the more I realized that the Bolsheviks had brought nothing to their country but misery, hunger and destitution.

On the way to Smolensk, we found quarters in a farmhouse, with very hospitable people who let us stay overnight. The whole family lived in one big room that had in its center a very large tiled oven with a dome. On the recess between the main part of the oven and the dome was a shelf, sleeping four. Mounted on a pole outside the house was a large tin can filled with water. A hole on the bottom was closed off with a rusty nail. When the nail was pushed up, a few drops of water would wet one's hands and it would be enough to sprinkle some water onto one's face.

Arriving in Smolensk, I was struck by this city's hilly terrain and by the many white-painted churches with gilded onion domes, glittering in the sun. But soon came my disappointment, as I found out that all these churches were used by the Soviets as stables, garages and warehouses.

We camped in front of a tall wall, which was part of the defenses used against Napoleon in the early 1800's. Not far from this wall was a building that housed a regiment of Russian soldiers consisting of all Jews recruited from the former Rumanian territories annexed by the Soviet Union.

They were very kind and tried to help us in any way they could. They took up a collection for us and would sneak us into their quarters after dark, so we were able to catch up on our sleep.

Soon the Soviet secret police found out about the foreigners hanging out at the Napoleonic wall and summoned us to appear at the headquarters of the NKGB (Narodny Komissariat Gosudarstvennoi Bezopasnosti — People's Commissar for State Security). After telling them we wanted to go to Moscow to see our ambassador, we were sent on our way accompanied by an armed "guide." We were put on a train and arrived at our destination in the morning.

The train pulled into the Byelo-Russky Wogsal, the White Russian railroad station. Masses of soldiers and civilians disembarked, rushing toward the exit. When the first onslaught was over, our escort guided us toward the exit and onto the streets of Moscow.

So this was the capital of the great Soviet Union, which had held fast in the face of vicious attacks by the Nazi forces? Moscow had driven the enemy back from its doorstep. Yet the eternal capital of world Communism now looked drab, colorless, monotone, even in the July sunshine — and so did the people.

Long lines in front of the bread stores indicated the shortness of supplies, which I found later was normal for the Russians. Moscow was a city in the midst of a war — tank traps on every intersection and anti-aircraft balloons strung in all parks and on the outskirts of the city. Cardboard or plywood substituted for broken window panes. Stovepipes peeked out of the openings cut into the windows, indicating that the lucky inhabitants had an oven for cooking and heat.

Here and there one could see the effects of the bombing raids, houses destroyed and the remaining walls reaching like gravestones into the sky.

What a contrast provided the Metro, the subway. The station we entered was decorated with red drapes and the floor covered with red carpets. An escalator led down to the platform, perhaps three to four stories below street level, with pictures decorating the walls on the side of the descending escalator. Arriving downstairs, the make-up of this station was really unbelievable. Arches leading from one side of the station platform to the other, with statues of Lenin, Stalin, Marx and Engels in white alabaster and crystal chandeliers hung from the ceilings. A clean and fairly modern subway train whisked us to our destination.

Upstairs the situation was quite different. We had to take a bus to wherever we were going. To our amazement, the bus was so crowded that people hung like grapes on every available step, bumper or whatever was protruding.

Apparently, we had arrived at our final destination and our accompanying Russian took us to a place that one only reads about in fairy tales. It looked like a castle, with manicured gardens and lawns, big fat people arriving in black limousines, dressed elegantly, the men wearing white slacks and blazers, some carrying tennis racquets. The women equally dressed in plain but rich elegance.

For the moment I believed, or wanted to believe, that this might just be the ideal place to spend the remaining war years. It did not look bad at all, but we would have to get new clothing in order to mingle with these elitist people.

My thoughts were cruelly interrupted when the doorman chased us angrily away, for this was the playground for the Kremlin crowd and was certainly not a hang-out for dirty refugees.

Krassnogorsk is a town less than ten miles outside Moscow. It is what would be called today a suburb, or a bedroom community. There were some dachas, industry and prisoner of war camps.

It was there, in full sight of Moscow, that the mighty German Army was beaten back. And it was there that the officer/musician who was to have led the marching band in the victory parade in Moscow was taken prisoner.

9. From being a Jew to being a German spy

And it was there that we were led into a building that housed the Communist Party and were taken in front of a Communist functionary for questioning.

After telling him that we had been imprisoned by the Germans because we are Jews and explaining our plan to find our ambassador-in-exile, he abruptly stopped our conversation cold. He informed us that the Soviets did not recognize our status as Jews. He said many so-called Jews who fled to the Soviet Union with "J's" in their passports were later discovered to be German spies. As far as the Soviet government was concerned, we were enemy aliens. Austria no longer existed, so we would be treated as German civilians and interned for the duration of the war.

This was the clincher. Under the Nazis, Jews were the enemy of the people — and here in the Soviet Union, where we thought to be free, we were branded as Germans and the enemy of the people.

We had to spend the night in this building. I remember sleeping on a bench no wider than perhaps eight inches. I woke up wondering why I had not fallen off.

The next morning, we were taken to a house that was really more a shack, right outside the prisoner of war compound. All seven of us were billeted in one room, just big enough to hold seven cots and one little table. The mattresses were jute bags filled with straw. Our freedom was limited and we were not allowed to leave a certain area.

A few days after our arrival in Krassnogorsk, the Soviet newspaper Pravda reported the finding of the concentration camp in Maly Trostenez. The Nazi murderers had brought thousands of people there at the last moment, killed them and piled the bodies crosswise in the large barns. Then they burned the barns along with the rest of the camp. All this took place about half an hour after we escaped.

The Veronal sleeping pills that each of us carried with the intent to kill ourselves in case of capture were used now to control the overpopulation of mice in our quarters.

After a few days of leisure, I was volunteered as a bookkeeper in the furniture factory within the prisoner of war compound. The man in charge of the factory, Ingber, was a Jewish prisoner of war from Hungary. Like so many of our co-religionists, he was conscripted by the Hungarian fascists into one of the slave labor battalions and sent to the Russian front, where he and the others were used to dig trenches and clear minefields. At the first possible moment they would escape to the Russian side, although in civilian clothing, where they were treated by the Soviets as enemies and taken prisoner.

The Hungarians had dismissed all Jews from military service at the onset of hostilities, but Jews who could prove they were officers in the Hungarian Army before the fascist takeover were afforded all privileges of their status.

We settled down to a routine. I was working in the furniture factory as the bookkeeper. My duties included keeping an eye on approximately 130 prisoners of war to see that they did their jobs correctly.

The Soviet system was built on the production level of the individual worker. If he produced more than the prescribed "norm," he would get a bonus. It was up to me to set the norm for the POWs. Their reward for exceeding it would be an extra piece of bread. Here I was faced with a dilemma. If I withheld the extra piece of bread as punishment, it would make me no better than the brutes I escaped from. On the other hand, we had to meet our quota. My way out was that I decided to play it exactly by the book. I set the norm in the morning and told them what I expected. In the evening I checked the production and gave each individual what he deserved. If he produced more than 100%, he was awarded the extra piece of bread. If he fell short, he did not receive the bonus. I tried to be fair throughout this ordeal.

I treated these people as human beings, unless I found out that one had belonged to the SS. Then my civility ceased and I would not rest until the Russians knew about it and would take care of that particular individual.

My knowledge of the Russian language was wobbly until I befriended a Russian officer who had been a professor of English at the University of Moscow. With my meager "school English," he was able to teach me Russian with English "subtitles." I was able to pick up basic Russian within a few weeks. My newly acquired vocabulary made it possible for me, to converse now in this complicated Slavic tongue.

I had an office in the furniture factory all to myself, until one day I was asked to share it with a watch repairman who had come from the part of Rumania occupied by the Hungarian fascists. Like all other Hungarian Jews, he had been forced to work in labor battalions, and as a result was taken prisoner by the Soviets.

On the frontline, as soon as a German surrendered or died, the Russian soldiers would take his watch. It was not unusual to see them walking around with four to five watches on each arm.

There was a case where a Russian brought a clock with a pendulum and wanted the watchmaker to "make three little ones" out of this monstrosity.

Within the prisoner of war compound there were a number of factories established and maintained by a Soviet trade organization. They, like any other undertaking in the Soviet Union, were owned by the Soviet government. Besides the furniture factory, there was a pottery, a blacksmith making ornate items, and a radio shop manufacturing radios that were in essence loudspeakers because all one could listen to was Radio Moscow. In charge of this production was a Lt. Movshovitz. Sitting in his office, with me at his side, he would summon one of the prisoners and ask him in a mixture of Yiddish and German if he needed anything. He would then suggest "maybe he could use socks or chocolate." The man would gladly agree to anything he was offered. With that, Movshovitz turned to me and said: "Seiler, write down that so-and-so wants socks and chocolate!" This was the end of the story, because the guy never received one or the other.

At another time, he asked me to come with him to "buy" lumber. I was dressed in a Russian uniform and wore a Finnish military coat. At the lumberyard, he introduced me as a "specialist from Czechoslovakia, who alone has the knowledge of 'correctly' measuring lumber." With my measuring and his sweet talk, we wound up with twice the amount of lumber we were entitled to.

My duties also included accompanying a working party of about 20 men to an aircraft factory about two miles outside the camp. I don't remember the kind of work these men had to perform, but I found it interesting to see that all machines in this plant were of Western origin.

Every day would bring a new experience, which in most cases would surpass the happenings of the previous day.

A new trade organization, led by a Jewish-Russian civilian, came to take over the factories. This group, also owned by the government, brought new machines and modern equipment to increase the production level.

But they had not counted on Movshovitz, who started to hide half of all items manufactured. Soon the new leader of this cartel came begging to Movshovitz to find out where the hidden items were.

One evening as I was leaving the bathhouse, I realized I had unwanted company to my right and to my left. Two policemen fell into step with me, guiding me to their headquarters, where I was questioned all night with bright lights focused into my eyes. All night I was told that "daylight you will never see again!" and that I was lying. A minimum incarceration or perhaps 10 years lay ahead of me. At three in the morning they let me go. (Thank you Comrade Movshovitz.)

Finally, the director of this new trade group decided he had enough of Movshovitz's shenanigans and that he would pull out of this mess. When the time came to pick up his machines, Movshovitz had buried them under the dirt floor of the diverse working places. (After I had left Moscow, I heard over the grapevine that Movshovitz was sentenced to ten years prison for his swindle.)

Winter had come almost overnight, with temperatures plunging way below zero and the landscape turning into a white, snow-covered fairy tale wonderland.

Nearly every night, after announcing a particular victory or the taking of a town, there would be a display of fireworks near the Kremlin, beautified by the reflection in the snow and ice and visible for miles.

The announcer, giving the news of the latest conquest on the radio-loudspeaker, would end with "death to the German occupiers." The report was signed by "Marshal J.V. Stalin."

Mid-winter I was approached to serve as an interpreter for the secret police. The work entailed the interrogation of prisoners of war to establish a permanent record and to find out more about each individual.

After a while, we learned exactly where what army was deployed and where each battalion was positioned and at exactly what time and where and when this particular person was taken prisoner. If the location of his army unit or the date and location of his capture did not correspond, we knew that this prisoner was lying and that we had to delve more into his past.

In questioning, we found a few soldiers who had belonged to the SS. We caught a man named Vierkant, who had been a member of the "SS Feldherrnhalle," an elite battalion that served directly under Hitler. We also caught an SS man named Voss, who had parachuted into Holland days before the invasion of that country and also landed in Norway as part of a fifth column weeks before the Germans came in force.

The POW hospital was staffed by three Hungarian-Jewish doctors. All three were fluent in their native tongue and in German and Yiddish.

Julie Hochbaum befriended one of these doctors, brought him to our lair and entertained him quite often, until he was arrested by the secret police. It turned out that he was neither a doctor nor a Jew. He wasn't even Hungarian. We found out that he was wanted in France for blowing up the harbor facilities in Marseilles without evacuating the civilian population. Thus he was guilty in the death of thousands of civilians.

The fireworks over Moscow were happening more frequently, with every display indicating the fall of another town or city, bringing the end of the war closer.

The German General Seidlitz Field Marshal von Paulus, (who had surrendered Stalingrad), the German poet Brecht and many other "big shot" Germans founded a "Free German Communist Government" in exile. They issued a newspaper, the "New Free Germany," and started to hold rallies with the POWs participating, trying to convert them to Communism.

10. Banished into the gulags

The war against Nazi Germany seemed to be going well, with the Red Army chalking up daily victories, when one morning in the latter part of March we were aroused by a knock on the door and told to pack. Within the hour, we were to be sent to a camp for civilian internees.

We packed our meager belongings and were given enough dried bread and salted dried fish for 10 days. Then we left under armed guard for Moscow.

There we made our way to the Kazan railroad station, only to find that the train we were supposed to take would not leave for two days. The station was an imposing edifice, with a large waiting hall filled with traveling soldiers and civilians waiting for their transportation and connections. Circles would build around Russians with accordions playing folk music, with people singing and dancing to these pleasant tunes. My sister, Yoshko and I would take short strolls, not to stray too far because of armed militia patrolling the streets and arresting any undocumented persons.

After two days of waiting, our train was ready to be boarded. To understand the make-up of the Russian rail system, one needs an explanation. Since the days of the Tsars, Russian rails have been set wider apart than West European or American rails. This was done to make it difficult for any conqueror to use Western rail equipment in occupying Russia. When the Germans started to wage war against the Soviet Union, they had to reset all rails to fit the

Western gauge. The railroad cars, therefore, were a little wider than their European cousins.

The inside of the rail cars looked very plain, with wooden benches facing each other. The Soviets had done away with first- and second-class cars, deciding that proletarians in a classless society don't have to sit on cushioned seats. On top of each set of benches was a shelf, perhaps originally planned for luggage but now used for people to lie on. In the middle of the wagon was an iron stove, radiating some warmth. In one corner of the railcar was a little compartment housing a couple who lived on the train and whose duty was to keep "their" car clean.

Between half the travelers spitting sunflower seed shells on the floor and the other half smoking *machorka* (a self-grown tobacco), the cleaning was no easy task.

As soon as the train left Moscow, I was amazed to see the vast expanses of the Russian plain, only here and there interrupted by small villages dotting the snow-covered landscape. Every time we encountered a train loaded with coal going west on a neighboring track, our train would stop. We would jump off to gather as much coal as possible to heat our rail car and also to add coal to the tender. (I was wondering if there was any coal left when the train reached Moscow).

Railroad stations are equipped with giant samovars, dispensing free boiling water to the weary traveler. At every stop, masses of people made a run for the water, using any available pot or can, often rushing back to a train already in motion. The boiling water was used to brew tea. If tea was not available, people just sipped the hot water and called it "white tea."

We passed through places like Gorky (Nishi Novgorod), Sverdlovsk (Ekaterinburg) and Kuybishev, winding through birch-tree forests and gradually ascending the Ural Mountains, the divide between Europe and Asia.

In Chelyabinsk in the Urals, we were scheduled to change trains to continue to Karaganda in the Soviet republic of

Kazakhstan.

Arriving in Chelyabinsk, we were told that the connecting train to our destination might be leaving in three to four days but this was not certain. Like so many others, we camped in the waiting room of the station.

The Urals are rich in ores and minerals, which is very important to the economy of the country. The mines were worked by imprisoned criminals living in forced labor camps — the gulags — or housed in the many jails all around Chelyabinsk.

Every day prisoners whose terms were up were released, resulting in a tremendous turnover. The newly released criminals would fall right back into their pattern and continued to ply their trade of robbing and plundering.

While scouting the area, I discovered the bazaar. The bazaar in Russia is a kind of open market place where an individual could rent a table for two rubles a day and sell either his self-grown produce or personal belongings.

Realizing this tremendous opportunity, I took the "delicious" dried salted fish, spread it on a waffle pique towel and went into the fish business. Every potential customer wanted to buy the towel, which was no bigger than a napkin, but nobody wanted to buy the fish (for which I couldn't blame them!). Just to get rid of the fish, I practically gave it away.

Next to me stood a Russian Jew, trying to sell a single rubber boot. Asked by another man in Yiddish what he was doing selling just one boot, he replied that "the other boot you'll find someplace else."

In Chelyabinsk, I saw for the first time in my life an "ice cream sandwich," two slabs of bread with a slice of frozen whipped cream in the middle.

On April 13, 1945 two important announcements were broadcast over the station's loudspeakers. The first was that President Roosevelt had died and an unknown, Harry Truman, had been sworn in as President of the United States. The second was that the capital of Austria, Vienna, had been conquered by Soviet forces. We had been waiting a long time for this, but instead of joy I felt depressed. Instead of traveling toward home, we were traveling east to a fate unknown. Instead of staying in Europe, we were exiled to Asia.

Kazakhstan

The Ural Mountains behind us, we traveled through the vastness of the Asiatic plains. Before we reached Karaganda, we passed through Petro-Pavlovsk, a major stop on the Southern branch of the Trans-Siberian rail, the first stop in Kazakhstan. There the train halted for about half a day. It gave me a chance to sell some undershirts and underpants that I had acquired in Moscow.

I had learned fast that in the Soviet Union there are two categories of jobs. The "warm" and the "cold" kind. A warm job means you can eat what you steal, and a cold job means you have to sell what you steal in order to buy something to eat.

I had three shirts on my arm when a Soviet officer, apparently a Kazakh, approached. He asked the price of the three shirts, which he then bargained down to half. Money changed hands. Later I returned with three pairs of underpants. When he expressed interest, I doubled the price on the underwear and he promptly bargained it down to half. After he paid, he turned back and said to me: "You are as clever as a Jew! What you didn't get on the shirts, you made up on the underpants!" (Little did he know that the Jew just took him!)

The landscape changed dramatically. Treeless flat savanna with no significant landmarks until we reached

Karaganda-Ugolnaya (Ugol means coal in Russian). There were active coal mines all around this Asiatic outpost in the Kazakhstan steppe, which looked like a town out of a Wild West saga.

The only significant difference was this plaza was obviously built to show the progress of Communism. A statue of Stalin stood in the middle of this square, surrounded by a few three-story apartment houses. The facades were painted in bright colors, with cows and goats on the balconies. The sides and rears of these houses were unpainted. Just past these buildings, the town simply ended. Beyond that was a desolate wasteland.

Kazakhstan steppe

We left on foot to be guided to a prisoner of war compound a few miles out of town to spend the night.

Our journey ended the next day when we were transported to another desolate outpost, Kok-U-Sek (coq-oo-sack), some 40 kilometers south of Karaganda. We joined other civilians, interned in a camp seemingly at the end of the world. Plateau and desert dominated the Republic of Kazakhstan, second in area to the Russian Federated Republic in the Soviet Union. The capital of Kazakhstan is Alma-Ata (today Almati), south of the mountains that stretch from east to west and divide the republic into two different climatic zones. While the territory to the south is blessed with permanent spring/ summer, the lands north of the divide, which include Karaganda, are open to severe winters with weather patterns emanating from the North Pole and from Siberia.

The summers are short, lasting perhaps four or five months, and are very hot and dry. Snowfall in the winter with drifts that sometimes reach 25 feet provides enough water when melted to fill three man-made lakes that supply irrigation for farmland.

To the south and east of Kok-U-Sek, a few hills dot the horizon, bringing some change and character to the land that greens only a short time after the melting of the snow. The change-over from winter to summer is sudden, with all the ice and snow melting in days, threatening to break the dams around the lakes. The runoff turns into a raging river.

Before the Bolshevik Revolution, the region around Kok-U-Sek was colonized by the British. The British were supposed to dig and export copper, but in reality they were exporting gold. They smelted the ore with coal carried from the pits in Karaganda via an existing rail line. The gold was sent out the same way. (The Brits were chased out after the revolution).

They also built sturdy, stone buildings topped with red tin that now housed 20,000 German and German-allied prisoners of war. The prisoner of war compound, like our civilian camp a short distance away, was surrounded by a 10-foot barbed-wire fence, with a five-meter strip of no-man's land on each side and watch towers every 50 or 75 meters.

It seemed like excess: Who could be stupid enough to try to escape when there was nowhere to go? China's Sinkiang province lay 600 kilometers east while India lay 1,500 kilometers south — and to get there, one would have to cross the Pamir highlands, and the foothills of the Himalayas.

The Reds had re-written the commandment dealing with the day of rest. In this new Communist Bible it said: "Six days shalt Thou labor for yourself and the seventh Thou shalt work without pay as a volunteer for the state."

This volunteer Sunday shall be known as Vosskressnik. On the first volunteer Sunday, the prisoners had to collect old iron. What better way was there to spend the day than to dismantle forty kilometers of rail from Kok-U-Sek to Karaganda?

The truck carrying us pulled into the camp gate to deposit us seven weary wanderers. I looked around wondering what the future held. Will we ever get out of this furthest removed outpost of humanity? Will anybody in this wide, wide world ever know anything about us? Or will we just disappear into the landscape, never to be seen or heard of again. God, is there a way out? Doubt had crept into my mind as to the good-will and the good intentions of the Soviets.

We were welcomed into the camp by a representative of the internees, who explained that this was a labor camp and that each of us would be given a job to perform.

About 800 people from all corners of Europe and all walks of life were in this camp. There were German Jews and Germans. Also Austrian Jews, who had escaped to Latvia and were interned by the Russians. And there were Spanish seamen and their officers who fought against Franco and brought a ship load of Spanish gold for safekeeping to the Soviet Union. The Russians confiscated the gold and imprisoned the crew.

There were Volga-Germans, who had settled in an autonomous territory granted them by the Empress Catherine, and there were Polish men, who had fought against the Nazis but did not volunteer to fight in the Polish Volunteer Corps.

There were people from Finland and Italy, from Yugoslavia and Rumania and Hungary, and even a few Armenians.

We did not get an extra day of rest to relax after our long journey. The morning after we arrived, my friend Yoshko and I were assigned to dig the foundation for a building to serve as a community hall dedicated to plays, dances, socials and political instructions. While I was digging with disgust, a tall man approached to ask whether the two of us understood anything about mechanics. I have never acquired a profession as fast as I did at that moment. He introduced himself as an engineer by the name of Siegel. He had originally come from Budapest, Hungary and had been in possession of an affidavit and visa to immigrate to the United States. The war in the Atlantic had dictated that the Siegels seek secondary ways of transportation to reach their destination. He, his wife and two sons received a transit visa to cross the USSR via the Trans-Siberian railroad, to catch a boat in Vladivostok to sail to the United States. It was June 22, 1941 when they were about to board the ship, the same day the Hungarians in concert with their German allies attacked the Soviet Union. The Russians had the whole family arrested and interned for the duration of the war and beyond.

We had to report to the command post the next morning, where we were met by engineer Siegel.

In order to leave the camp outside of a working party, as an individual assigned to a specific task, one had to get political clearance. Then you were given a number engraved on a metal tag. While passing through the command post, the tag was to be moved from the "in camp" board to the "out of camp" board. In entering the camp, the procedure was reversed.

The lakes that held the irrigation water were called *platinas*. The largest had a unique way of withdrawing water and pumping it into the irrigation canals using a siphon. A large pipe about two feet in diameter was laid across the dam, with one end reaching deep into the water and the other end open toward the land. Both ends were closed off with shut-off valves, while four men pumped water into the pipe through a small opening on the top. When the pipe was filled, the valves were opened simultaneously and water would flow freely, until stopped by closing one of the valves.

The second dam was called the small platina, which served a very limited area by way of a mechanical pump.

The third, or the new platina, was equipped with a wooden bridge as walkway and had a large Russian-made motor from the year 1911 to drive the pump. This pump station is where our new friend had brought us. He explained that we had to start the pump every morning at 4:30, so there would be enough water in the canals when the women come out at 6:00 a.m. to irrigate the fields.

He explained also how to start this motor, which he said was very simple. Just take off the iron head of the engine, put the head into the fire that you have made out of little twigs and grasses that you will find all around in the taiga (steppe). Meanwhile, make putty by mixing asbestos with water and put it around the rim, where the head is going to rest. When the head is red and glowing, pick it up with the tongs, tighten it fast, turn the swing wheels and presto — the motor runs!

Engineer Siegel also put me in charge of the kerosene supply necessary to operate the engine and the pump. He told me where to go and whom to see.

The next day, I made my way to the den of the "dragon." His name was Nestrov, and he was in charge of the bakery and of petroleum supplies. When I entered his office, he was sitting behind his desk in a shabby, crumpled-up uniform, two sizes too big, his military cap sitting on the back of his head. His boots, which had seen better days, were much too large for a man not even five feet tall. I had addressed him as "Comrade Nestrov," but he immediately corrected me. He was not my "comrade." I was to address him as "Citizen Nestrov." That was fine with me. Who wanted to be a "comrade" to this little Caesar? I told him I had come to pick up a barrel of kerosene. At that moment I thought the world had come to an end. He ranted and raved for a good ten minutes before he released the barrel of kerosene into my care. His men loaded it onto a horse-driven cart that I drove out to the platina. That was just the first of my many run-ins with Nestrov, which occurred whenever I needed kerosene. Later when I was in charge of the power station, he went into such frenzies that I thought the man would have a heart attack every time.

We learned fast. First of all, the question of making fire – with what? Matches were not easily obtainable, and seldom ignited in any case. The typical Russian method was to hit a piece of steel against a rock, catching a spark on a wick or on a piece of cotton torn out of ones jacket lining. Then you'd blow at the glowing wick or cotton ball and try to ignite a piece of paper or a bunch of dry grasses. This was not my cup of tea.

We decided, like Prometheus, to bring the fire with us — not from heaven, but from the camp kitchen. We chainsmoked all the way from the camp to the platina. With the glimmer from the cigarettes and with some wood expropriated from the bridge, we got the fire going and the motor to run. (By the time the season was over, half the bridge had gone up in smoke).

Later in the season, we stole vegetables and melons from the fields to supplement our daily diet. (I would go out early in the morning, get our supplies for the day and run back through the canals, before the water started to flow. To get caught meant 10 days in jail).

On the 8th day of May 1945, the Soviets declared a special holiday. The war in Europe was over.

The whole camp population congregated in an open field, amid music and flags while Russian politicos spoke in glowing terms of how the Communist forces alone had delivered the death blow to the German Nazi devils. One political orator followed another — never even mentioning the Western powers — about what this victory meant to Bolshevism and to Mother Russia. Suddenly and without any idea on my part, the Politrook (political teacher) called on Yoshko Pollack to speak. My mouth fell open. I was listening to my friend of many years, and I did not recognize this person. He stood there with his fist raised in Communist salute, reciting his belief in the Communist cause, delivering a declaration of his own Bolshevik manifesto.

I continued working with Yoshko, but from then on, always being aware of his leanings and avoiding any conversation that could be interpreted as a political statement.

I did not want to sound ungrateful — yes, the Soviets had saved my life — but at the same time, I really did not want to overstay my welcome. If it were up to me, they could have sent me home right there and then.

In the beginning of September, we dismantled the pump station and moved the motor and the pump into a workshop in the POW compound, for overhaul and rehabilitation. We received special permission to enter and leave the POW camp at will. We intended to hibernate in our workshop, with practically nothing to do.

In the beginning of 1946, I was selected to assist another mechanic, Pavel, in running the power station for the whole area. The power net supplied our camp, the POW camp and the "free" Russian village. My co-worker Pavel was a Volga-German, born in Russia, where his family had lived for generations but never opted for Russian citizenship. When Pavel was sent to another job, I was put in charge of the power station to supply electric power from dusk until two in the morning.

Walking back to the camp at that hour, especially in the winter with the mercury at 40 degrees below zero, was an unbelievably eerie experience. The air was crisp and clear, the stars seemed close enough to be touched and the reflection of the ice toward the sky created a vision of five moons. Gathered on the horizon was a pack of wolves howling, their tracks crisscrossing my footprints in the icy snow. My frozen breath clung to my nostrils and eyebrows and at times made the walk home difficult: I had to climb down on one side of the embankment of the now dried-up creek and scramble up the other. Coming close to the camp, my presence was challenged by the soldiers in the watchtowers, who yelled, "Halt, who goes?"

My position, though, brought a lot of privileges. For a bottle of kerosene, I would be fed in the camp kitchen "real" food at two in the morning. In the bathhouse, where one had to report to every 10 days, I could have as many barrels of hot water (the size of a pail) as I wanted, not just one. In the barracks, when they doled out the soup three times a day, I could have the thick part, which I refused.

My position also allowed me to hang out next door in the "free" Russian hospital, with which the power station shared one building. I befriended the chief doctor. Doctor Lastochkin confided in me that the reason he was exiled from Moscow was that he asked in a circle of friends, "What did Trotsky really do?" For this he got 10 years jail and interior exile to Siberia. "You know," he once told me, "that in my house, the servants used to wear white gloves while serving dinner." It also gave me an opportunity to meet and make the acquaintance of a number of Russians who for one or other reason wound up in this God-forsaken corner of the earth.

I suppose the uncertainty and hopelessness that had spread throughout the camp was the reason that morals and decency, with very few exceptions, had completely broken down. One-night stands were the order of the day, and new couples were forming and breaking up incessantly. Masses of babies showed no resemblance to their legal fathers. It seemed that Sodom and Gomorrah had risen from the ashes.

Most of the camp's male population was involved digging up the oxygenated coal leftovers from the smelters that the Brits had dumped all over the landscape. This "coal" was used now for cooking and heating the barracks — and all this only 40 kilometers from one of the richest coal deposits in the Soviet Union.

The Spanish seamen braided upper parts for women's shoes out of some white strings that the camp commando supplied. The Polish men were involved in erecting buildings, using unburned bricks called *saman* that were made by mixing clay with straw and dried in the sun. They used the same method as the Israelites in Egypt. The only difference is that a span of oxen did the actual mixing; they were hitched to a beam, which was hooked in the center to an open round pit in an arrangement that resembled a Mixmaster.

In summer, the women's job was to irrigate the fields and after harvest time, to clean, assort and keep the vegetables dry and clean in the cellars. Certain vegetables were pickled or preserved in other ways.

A Dr. Winter from Vienna was in charge of the camp hospital, assisted by a very capable nurse and by his wife, who would occasionally fly by on her broom.

The clinic was run by "Feldsher" Herrig — a Feldsher is a person, who is as knowledgeable as a doctor, but does not have a degree — who eventually cured my furunculosis, which had covered most of my lower body.

Twice a year, around the beginnings of May and November, the Russians would raid the barracks, go through one's personal belongings and confiscate anything they considered counterrevolutionary, illegal or unnecessary. At one of these raids, they had taken away a framed picture of Stalin that I had received as a gift in Moscow, and for which I really did not care. But they had also taken my spare pair of shoes, which they deemed to be unnecessary. The boots I had been wearing since we left Vienna showed signs of age. I went down to the command post to re-claim my possession and face the commandant of the camp, Matyushin. He was a typical Russian muzhik, with a big mustache and stocky build who always walked like a drunk. "What is it you want?" he roared. I complained: "You took my shoes," and he countered: "And what is it you wear?" "These are my own boots," I answered. He replied: "Nothing is your own! Everything belongs to the state. You belong to the state, your boots belong to the state." Then, referring to the male sex organ, he added, "and this belongs to the state too!" With that my audience had ended. For better or worse, winter or summer, I had only one pair of boots.

Smirnoff was the Soviet officer in overall charge of the power station. His personal life was a mystery to me. He never spoke of anything or mentioned anybody and seldom visited the station. It surprised me when he walked in one night, totally drunk, and started to cuss the leadership of the Soviet Union. Starting with Stalin, calling him a murderer and a no good son-of-a-bitch, down to the last local Communist political commissar. They were all criminals, not worthy to lead the country nor to live. When he showed up the next evening, he wanted to know, if he was here the previous night and if he had said anything. I answered in the positive and told him that he had spoken up. Needless to say, that from that time on, we became good friends.

One week before the Japanese surrendered to the American forces, the Russians declared war on the Japanese Empire and occupied Manchuria. There, Japan's Kwantung Army surrendered to the Soviets, along with all its equipment .

Some of these new prisoners of war were sent to the existing POW camp next door to ours. The Russians let the Japanese officers keep their cold weapons, until one of their prisoners was caught stealing bread from his comrade. As punishment and in front of the whole assembly, the Japanese officer had the soldier kneel down, drew his saber and chopped off the man's head. (Needless to say, the Russians took away the officers' swords and knives).

We needed a new motor to drive the dynamo in the power station, so we decided to take one of the Japanese truck's diesel engines and make it stationary by securing it on a frame firmly attached to the ground. In looking for the right engine, we were amazed to find that we had to combine parts of three different engines because the Japanese had sabotaged the equipment before surrendering.

To discuss certain problems that we faced, we usually met with the officers and mechanics to figure out a solution. For instance, with the motor taken from the Japanese trucks, we would crouch in a circle. One of the men would bring out a piece of lard, cut it in pieces and hand each one of us a piece. Then the bottle of home-brewed vodka would make the rounds, followed by a slice of onion. (It is better to smell of onion, than of vodka!)

To get a frame in a hurry, we had to "borrow" one from the new platina, where we had no use for it through the winter months. Snow was already on the ground when we took a horse driven sled to dismantle the frame and bring it to the station. Successfully and without a hitch, we installed the new motor and were able to continue operating the station without interruption.

Soon the winter of 1946-47 had come with a fury. The big danger lay in violent snow storms, called burans. In a buran, the snow was being twisted and twirled, like the dust in a tornado. If one was unlucky enough to be caught in a storm like this, it was very easy to lose direction and freeze to death, as happened to two Russian on the way to their barracks.

In the beginning of 1947, we were notified that a spare frame would be available, if we could get it right away. The weather was not too bad yet, so we decided to take a chance and get this frame, before it disappeared. We hitched a couple of horses to a sled and off we went to Karaganda, some forty kilometers away. The trip to the city went comparatively fast and we were able to make the deal with the Kazakh man who "owned" this piece of equipment in a short time. After that, my companion and I went to the bazaar to buy some odds and ends.

There was an elderly man selling salamis. Luckily, he pointed out that these salamis were made out of cat. My travel companion bought some "self-brewed" vodka, which the seller was obligated to sip first to make sure the vodka was not poison. We also bought some tobacco, which was sold by the glassful and poured directly into one's pants pockets.

It was already late afternoon and dark when we started

on our journey back. My special five moons escorted us most of the way, and in this crystal clear night, the temperature dropped way below zero. We struggled along, most of the time running next to the sled to keep warm. Then, getting too tired to run further, we would sit a while on the sled, then run again, while it got colder by the second. We reached Kok-U-Sek at sunrise, when through the reflection on the icy surface, we observed three red suns rising on the horizon.

I always had problems taking off my boots and most of the time needed help. This time they nearly fell off my feet, revealing white toes. The men in my barrack picked me up and carried me into the hospital, where I was found to have frostbite on five of my toes. The people there were successful in saving them. I remained in the hospital about four or five weeks, until I had a disagreement with the head nurse, when I refused to eat a soup made out of sour pickles, which was not fit for human consumption. She maintained that if I was well enough to refuse to eat, I was well enough to get out of the hospital.

I was detailed to do light work and was sent to the shoe-repair shop. Overnight, I graduated to become a shoe repairman and shoemaker.

Toward the end of the year, a group of about two hundred, mostly Viennese Jews who had originally fled the Nazis and emigrated to Riga, Latvia, was sent home. From then on, whenever we encountered officers or higher brass, we would query them as to when our turn would come to be released. Most of the time, we were met by cold stares. (Matyushin, our commandant, would say: "Foolish people, why would you want to go home? Here you get three times soup a day and in Europe, the potatoes are as expensive as eggs here!")

Letters that we tried to mail to the Austrian ambassador in Moscow probably never left the censor's office. As time went on and we did not get anywhere, desperate and frustrated, we organized and called a hunger strike. We demanded a commission be sent from Moscow to look into our unjust detention, nearly two years after the end of the war. After the third or the fourth day of the strike, the commission that came was not interested in our complaints. They just wanted to find the culprit who organized this "counter-revolutionary" strike. Not able to find the guilty party, they arrested three of our people at random and put them, dressed only in their underwear, into solitary confinement.

Meanwhile, the Russians ordered the camp kitchen to bake cake and cookies. The odor of these baked goodies permeated the camp. We lost a few strikers, but the majority held fast.

On the seventh day, we negotiated a truce: As soon as our three men were returned, we would end the strike.

Winter had yielded again to warm weather when I was summoned by Matyushin to report to the command post. He asked me to take control and oversee the work at the three pumping stations. According to my medical record, my frostbitten toes (and my personally being acquainted with the Russian chief doctor), my status was like "4F" (light duty only). I did not have to accept any job outside the confines of the camp. When I initially refused, he got wild, screaming and yelling that this was what the "elders" had taught me and that my actions were counter-revolutionary. This was not the Communist way. When the party calls, when the state needs you to volunteer your services, you go and do your duty, and so on.

Then, he gave me until two in the afternoon to change my mind. After some more pressure from Matyushin and the labor inspector, Germanovskaya, a Russian/Jewish woman, I reconsidered. I accepted the position, which I calculated would leave me free to roam the countryside at will, telling the people at every pump station that I would be at the other.

In the early part of the summer, as long as the grasses were still fresh, I liked to disappear into the hills, marvel at the flowers that came in all colors of blues, blacks and greens and dotted the landscape. I would take long rests stretched out under the sunny sky, with my cap serving as a pillow, only to discover once that a snake had taken refuge under it.

I made the acquaintance of some Khazak shepherds who lived in earthen dugouts, called *semlyankas*. A semlyanka was a hole about 12 feet by 12 feet, about six to seven feet deep and with a roof, adding about two feet above the ground. In winter, these semlyankas kept the warmth and in summer they were naturally air-conditioned. In the middle of this below-surface place, on the earthen ground, was an open fire. A tray-like platform, standing on ornate legs, served for cooking. A roasted sheep was eaten by all present, sitting on the floor in a circle and ripping pieces of the sheep with their hands, or fingers. This meal was called *beshbarmak* (five fingers). To wash it down, they served kumiss, fermented horse's milk that could get one easily drunk.

1947 was also the year of the locust. They came by the millions, the swarms moving and driven by the wind, darkening the sun. Each had a wingspan of about five inches and a saw-like tooth protruding about one inch. Our defense consisted of barrels of burning petrol set around the fields and an army of volunteers hitting the locusts with wet rags. Still, thousands of those pink monsters settled on the plants and destroyed acres of vegetation. When the wind picked up and carried them away, we hoped that it should not shift again and bring back this biblical plague.

The pumps folded in early fall and I oversaw the removing and storing of the machinery. A number of our men went to see the commandant, Matyushin, to ask for a day off for the highest Jewish holiday, Yom Kippur. After twirling his mustache for a while, he came up with a brilliant solution. Our people should postpone Yom Kippur to the "October Revolution Holiday," which was actually celebrated in November, based on the old Russian-Orthodox calendar. Then, he said, we will celebrate together.

The seasons turned again and the cold weather set in, registering the first snowfall in early October. We got ready for another year of suffering, when in the beginning of December 1947, eleven of us were notified, that we would to be released and sent home.

11. Going home

On December 2, 1947 we got the order to pack our belongings and report to the community hall outside the camp that served the "free" Russian population. We were not permitted to re-enter the camp. I used the opportunity to visit my nemesis, Nestrov. He was in his office when I entered and told him that I came to say good-by to him. He said: "So what?" I said "Comrade, you don't understand, I am going home — but you, you are going to stay here." With that, and a big smile, I left him to his thoughts.

We were told that we were going to leave the next morning. We were quartered in this large, unheated community hall when suddenly a side door opened and in walked Maria Ilonovna, the wife of the political commissar. She had come to take me and my family into her husband's warm and heated office to spend the night. She appeared again the next morning. With a gesture of love representing the free Russian population, she handed me a loaf of bread and a cellar of salt as gift.

On the 4th of December, we were loaded on a freight train, attached to the 36th POW transport being sent home. The following day we left Karaganda for good. Dreamlike, the names of towns and villages whisked by the speeding train: Orsk, near Saratov, where we crossed the Volga, which is at this point four kilometers wide; Kursk, Kiev, Kolomea and finally crossing the border into Rumania, at Marmorosz-Sziget. The border itself was like the barbed-wire and watchtower set-ups of a concentration camp. The Russians had all the prisoners of war de-train. They had to remove their shirts and walk by a commission with their arms raised. Here we found out that SS men had their blood types tattooed under their arms. A number of former SS men were removed from this transport.

It was the 25th day of December when we arrived in this border town in Rumania. A sudden thaw melted the snow and created a high-water situation in the valley between the Carpathian Mountains, swelling the Theiss (Tissa) river and tearing away the only rail road bridge leading out of this nest.

We were billeted in a rat-infested former Rumanian army base, and the remaining Jewish population of Sziget provided us with food daily. On January 1, 1948 we were made aware of the abdication of King Michael of Rumania in favor of the Communist dictator, Petru Grosza. The Russians had all along maintained a strong presence in this now Communist state. When Rumanian army personnel encountered Russians on the streets, they spat on the ground instead of saluting.

Toward the end of February, the rail bridge was repaired and we left on the 20th of that month on the last leg of our journey. For 150 kilometers, we had to travel through Soviet territory, during which time the train was sealed. Near Chop, we crossed into Hungary and on the 21st of February 1948 after leaving Hungary at Sopron, we were welcomed into Austria, by a commission in Wiener Neustadt.

12. Home at last

Finally, put on a passenger train and passing by long for-gotten names of towns and villages like Bad Vöslau, Baden, at long last we arrived in the city of my birth, Vienna.

"Blessed art Thou, o Lord our God, King of the Universe, who has kept us in life and hast sustained us and enabled us, to reach this time." —A Hebrew blessing.

It was early evening when the train pulled into the Southern Rail terminal that still showed the destruction caused by war. The once magnificent hall had no roof and some parts of the walls had disappeared. People were mill-ing around, waiting and hoping that this train from the Soviet Union would bring their dear ones back from exile, back from one of the hundreds of prisoner of war camps that dotted Russia. Each wanted to be first to greet and hug them, and welcome them back after their ordeal.

Others were holding up pictures or just signs with the names of soldiers with the big question: "Have you seen so and so?" Some said, "Missing in action," hoping for a miracle, that someone would say: "Yes I have seen him," or, "Yes, this person is alive".

Darkness had fallen rather quickly by the time we de-trained. All eleven of us were met by representatives of the Jewish Community Council (Kultusgemeinde) and guided to a waiting van to be taken to quarters provided by the city of Vienna.

The moment I had so intently prayed for, this moment, beyond belief, had finally arrived. Finally and unconditionally we are free, free, free.

The van started out toward the 19th district. We passed only one block away from my birth-house in the Kurzgasse. I asked the driver to stop for a moment while I stepped out of the van to look at this unbelievable sight: Here washed by the moonlight was the house I was born in.

The circle was completed. My odyssey of 10 years almost to the day had come to an end. I had survived but at what cost? When all this started I was a boy. I had returned as a man.

They had stolen my youth. They had stolen 10 years of my life.

Epilogue

I had been a slave laborer in German and Soviet prisons and camps, yet I deemed myself lucky — luckier than the six million of my people who had not survived. Luckier than some of the citizens of all nations — neutrals, allied or in the enemy camp — who had been killed on the front lines or disappeared in the gulags in the perma-frozen tundras of Siberia, never to be seen or heard from again.

The truth about the Nazi concentration camps became public knowledge. Some of the Nazis, guilty of war crimes, were apprehended. Some committed suicide, some were caught years later and brought to justice and some were never found.

Dr. Heuser, the Nazi prosecutor of Minsk, turned up the last day at the Maly Trostenez camp. He collected the two women he had originally brought there from the Minsk ghetto and left with them in his private car. According to newspaper reports, he was sentenced to fifteen years imprisonment for his participation in the Nazi affairs of Minsk. Perhaps the two women saved him from a more severe sentence.

Let this document stand as a reminder of man's inhumanity to man. Of what, when unleashed, man is capable of inflicting onto others. Of what hatred, state-induced and state-controlled, can do.

Safeguard these written words and hand them down to generations yet unborn.

The question that I encountered often was: "In all this, where was God?"

To which I had to answer, with a question of my own: "Where was Man?"

13. The years that followed

WORLD WAR II had finally come to an end. The symbol of the Nazis, the ugly swastika that stood for racial hatred, now lay broken on the ground for everyone to step and spit upon.

Sieveringer Hauptstrasse 245

The Jewish community of Vienna had been reduced from 185,000 to approximately 7,000 souls and was looking for a new beginning. People who had returned were quartered in former Jewish villas and palaces until they found living quarters. We were sent to a building in Döbling at 245 Sieveringer Hauptstrasse to be used as our temporary abode.

I found myself in the city of my birth, a city now partially destroyed, showing its war wounds and occupied by the four allied victors: The United States, Great Britain, France and Soviet Russia. The occupying forces were constantly patrolling the streets of the city; while you felt secure in those controlled by the Western powers, you felt always uneasy in the Soviet zones.

An incident occurred that made me realize that perhaps

it would be better for me to leave Austria. I was threat-ened by three Soviet soldiers and had to take refuge in the Grand Hotel in Meidling, which was flying the British flag. My thoughts at that time were that wherever Ivan puts his boot print, he will never remove it. I must admit that at that time I was mistaken: Ivan the Terrible left Austria in 1955.

Franz Josef Kai, 1949

I found employment with the AJDC, the American Joint Dis-tribution Committee, which was established to help new immi-grants and emigrants with food and clothing. I was there until I left for the United States at the end of 1949, helped by my father's friend Wolko Schmetterling, who was kind enough in issuing an affidavit for the whole family. He was the owner of a retail clothing shop in Philadelphia who came to the States in 1938.

Emil

Leafing through the book of times, I came across an interesting story that sometimes escapes one's eyes.

My father met his childhood friend and next-door neighbor Emil Linden-feld-Sommerstein from the town of Kopczynce, in front of the school they were attending. Unknown to them, they were registered in the same pub-lic school.

They grew up in Vienna, near one another, knew about one another, but never resumed their childhood closeness. Emil Lindenfeld-Sommerstein married Lydia Lindenfeld, nee Sturm, the daughter of a "Posamentrie" owner, the maker of fancy table cloths, coverlets and such. Lydia's father had a large factory in Jägersdorf in the Sudentenland.

Lydia

Their marriage produced one daughter, Alice Lindenfeld. When the Hitler hordes occupied Austria, Alice was sent to England with one of the famous Kinder Transports. By a lucky coincidence, her mother, Lydia, was able to obtain a working permit as a domestic and followed her daughter to England. They survived unharmed through The Blitz, the German bombardment of London.

Emil was able to stay in Vienna during the Nazi occupation as a "U-Boat," hiding out with non-Jewish relatives and friends. Alice's parents never reunited and the father continued living in Vienna.

June 17, 1951

Before settling in the United States, Alice came to visit her father and to meet with me and my family. Out of this meeting, came a promise to keep in touch in the U.S. and which led eventually to an engagement. After living in Philadelphia for one year, I moved to New York to settle and to get married. Our marriage took place in Kew Gardens Hills on the 17th of June 1951, officiated by Rabbi I. Usher Kirshblum.

I started working in the textile field in Midtown Manhattan, for low wages and long hours. I worked hard and diligently and was rewarded with

Sandra and Howard, 1958

wage increases, so I could see a promising future ahead.

To our joy, we welcomed our daughter Sandra on August 27, 1952. Five years later, on November 14, 1957 our son Howard arrived.

My parents, my sister Mary and her husband Kurt, remained in Philadelphia running a clothes manufacturing company under the name of Seiler & Weisz.

Mary and Kurt were married in Philadelphia, May 1951 and had two girls, Debbie (Deborah) and Bibi (Beatrice).

My parents, sister Mary and Mary's daughters Debbie and Bibi

Grandmother And Girl Killed In Midcity Fire

Child and 2 Women Trapped on Landing Of Arch St. Building

Mrs. Clara Seiler, 65, died to-day of burns from a fire from which she tried vainly to save her little granddaughter.

The child, Beatrice Weisz, five, was burned to death at 3.35 yesterday afternoon when flames swept a four-story build-ing at 923 Arch st.

She, her grandmother and her mother had found refuge on the second floor landing of an out-side fire escape.

Flames roaring along the first floor burst through a sidewalk display window, sprang upward

Brit To For

Loophole Pr

Tax-W For Di

Washington, 24
—The Kennedy
tion's nominee
chief in the Tre
possibility of ins
tem of withhold
dividend and Inte

All seemed to be going well for all the families when tragedy struck

On March 23rd 1961, an explosion and fire ripped apart a display dealer's plastic supply business in a four-story building at 923 Arch Street. My parents' factory was in the same building

My mother, my sister, my niece Bibi and other employees were killed.

I was offered a partnership in an import/export textile house, a business career that I pursued incessantly. We were very successful until the Chinese manufactures entered and controlled the market place.

My daughter Sandra, nee Seiler, married Stewart Garfinkel on June 28th 1981. They are the parents of Jaclyn, born February 20, 1985, and Alison, born on May 28, 1988.

Sandra's family in 2003

Howard's family in 2003

My son Howard and his wife Lenora, nee Novello, married on December 28, 1990. They have two children. Joshua was born on February 7, 1993 and their daughter Leah arrived on October 11, 1996.

On May 21, 1985, after suffering for a long time from breast cancer, Alice, my wife of 34 years, succumbed to the disease.

They say that sometimes when a door closes, another opens.

In February 1986, while I was on one of my visits to the Metropolitan Museum of Art in New York, I met and befriended a lady who became my future wife. We had common roots, as she originated from Vienna as well. On July 19, 1988 Margarete Auguste Seiler,

Greta and Fred in 2006

nee von Schenkenbach and I tied the knot.

Our family grew with the addition of her son Christopher Garrett and his wife, Lucia; and her daughter Carol Kaimis with her husband Kyriacos (a.k.a. Charlie) and their two children, Alexandra and Christiana.

Credits

I have tried to tell my story against the backdrop of major events in contemporary world history and have tried to describe the moments of terror and despair and the moments of elation, to the best of my ability.

I have used the following publications for correctness of dates:

Die Chronik Österreichs, by Prof. Walter Keindel
The Minsk Ghetto, by Hersen Smolar
....and God Cried, by Charles Lawless

At this time I want to express my gratefulness and my thanks for the tremendous editing job of my wife Margarete Seiler, nee von Schenkenbach, and her granddaughter Toya Margaret Brown.

Postscript by Margarete Seiler

Upon retirement in 2000, my husband Fred and I moved to West Palm Beach, Florida. He became a member of Temple Sinai in Delray Beach, Florida and there he continued his work educating those he met about the history and background of Nazi Germany and the ultimate atrocity of the Holocaust.

As he did at the Temple of Kew Garden Hills in New York, Fred continued to lead the Yom Hashoah services at Temple Sinai as well. He was a proficient speaker, relaying his experiences in a beautiful and clear voice. When he spoke on the occasion of remembrance for the six million Jews whose deaths at the hands of the Nazi regime are known as the "Shoah," one could hear a pin drop. His deliverance was always riveting and eloquent. He had lived the nightmare.

**Robert Marchl
interview 2005**

Fred and I traveled the world together. On one particular visit to Austria, we were contacted by a young man from Graz, Robert Marchl. While studying and working in Minsk,

Belarus, Robert became aware of the existence of a former German concentration camp in the area named Maly Trostenez. Although thousands of Viennese Jews perished there and only a few survived, the camp was practically

unknown outside of the area. Robert intended to write a book on Maly Trostenez and for two consecutive years he met with us to record Fred's experiences. My husband expressed his wish to one day return to the camp for closure.

At the place of deportation, the train station in Vienna

This wish became a reality when Robert Marchl contacted a well-known producer, Dr. Andreas Gruber. Mr. Gruber became interested in filming Fred's story. In the spring of 2007 Robert and his crew, Matthias and Stefan, arrived in Florida to film some preliminary footage.

At the end of August 2007, accompanied by my step-son Howard, we flew first to Vienna to meet Mr. Gruber and start the filming. A few days later, at the invitation of the Belarus government, we all flew to Belarus (White Russia) so Fred might finally be able to find his closure. The day we drove to the former concentration camp in Maly Trostenez was, appropriately, a cold and rainy one reminiscent of the cold bitterness and tears of the many who had died there.

Whether or not Fred had ever really found closure at this visit is truly unknown to me.

The next day in Minsk, Fred was invited to speak at the opening ceremony of the History Workshop in the former Minsk Ghetto. There, a photo exhibition was displayed paying homage to the memory of the many murdered children in the death camps. The dedication was covered by both radio and television crews. Many illustrious and well-known personalities of Europe were present as well. Leonid Levin, a well-known White Russian architect, recipi-

ent of the Lenin Medal and the creator of the memorial "Krasnyj Bereg" (Red Shore), was the speaker at the ceremony. I quote Mr. Levin's address to my husband from the Minsk newspaper: "Mr.

Speaker Leonid Levin

Seiler, I cannot tell you 'thank you' for what you went through and that you looked death into the eye," said Leonid Levin in his appreciation to the Austrian guest, who came despite his medical problems to Minsk. "I can only say that in the same way and manner, for many of us the war until today still exists: because our fathers did not return from the front and the mothers wait in vain for their sons..."

In the former Jewish ghetto cemetery in Minsk, there are few memorials to the remembered murder victims. The memorials that are erected are dedicated to all who died at the hands of the Nazis but there is not one specifical-

Memorials at the former Jewish ghetto cemetery

ly from Austria commemorating the memory of the approximately 10,000 Viennese Jews who perished there.

Robert Marchl and a group of dedicated people are working to get the authorities to erect a memorial in their honor.

Interview with Dr. Enigl

Upon our return to Vienna, Fred was interviewed by Dr. Marianne Enigl of the prestigious Austrian publication, PROFIL. The article appeared in the magazine on November 19, 2007 and was entitled, "Immer noch weglaufen" (still running away). Ms. Enigl took the idea from a comment Fred had made during the interview when he remarked, "In my nightmares I am still in the camp and I must still run away."

**PROFIL
November 19, 2007**

Included in the article were facts and statistics about the deportation of Viennese Jews. Ms. Enigl writes, "The first deportation took place at the end of November 1941 and nine more followed between May and October 1942. Each transport consisting of approximately 1,000 victims. Aside from the ten transports from Vienna, Jews from the Minsk Ghetto, deportees from different German cities and thousands of Russian prisoners of war

134

were brutally murdered at Maly Trostenez. The investigating Soviet commission in 1944 estimated a total of 200,000 victims."

At the time of filming, Fred was one of three survivors still living. According to Russian documents, within hours of the escape of the 17 survivors, some 4,000 victims were murdered by the Germans in a last-minute killing frenzy.

In the spring of 2008, the documentary of my husband's journey to Minsk and Maly Trostenez, "Aus dem Paradies zurück zur Hölle" (From Paradise Back to Hell), was broadcast a number of times on the Austrian public TV channel ORF. As ill as Fred was at the time, he was ever so grateful to Robert, Dr. Gruber, his staff and all who were partners in delivering the truth about the atrocities at Maly Trostenez thereby memorializing the souls of those who never made it out.

Surrounded by his family and reciting the Shema, Fred left this life on July 20, 2008 with his legacy finally realized. Fred knew that he had done everything possible to ensure that the "Shoah" would never fade from the memory of humankind.

Afterword

On September 18, 2009, 64 years after the liberation, the Austrian government finally unveiled a memorial stone at the former Minsk ghetto cemetery dedicated to the memory of the more than 9,600 murdered Austrian Jews at Maly Trostenez.

Printed by Amazon Italia Logistica S.r.l.
Torrazza Piemonte (TO), Italy

68184663R00084